OTHER BOOKS BY NICK VUJICIC

Life Without Limits

Unstoppable

Limitless

New York Times and International Best-Selling Author of *Unstoppable*

NICK VUJICIC

STAND
STRONG

You Can Overcome Bullying
(and Other Stuff That Keeps You Down)

WATERBROOK
PRESS

STAND STRONG
PUBLISHED BY WATERBROOK PRESS
12265 Oracle Boulevard, Suite 200
Colorado Springs, Colorado 80921

Details in some anecdotes and stories have been changed to protect the identities of the persons involved.

Trade Paperback ISBN 978-1-60142-782-3
Hardcover ISBN 978-0-307-73093-0
eBook ISBN 978-0-307-73094-7

Cover design by Kristopher K. Orr; cover photography by Mike Heath, Magnus Creative

Published in the United States by WaterBrook Multnomah, an imprint of the Crown Publishing Group, a division of Penguin Random House LLC, New York.

WATERBROOK and its deer colophon are registered trademarks of Penguin Random House LLC.

The Library of Congress has cataloged the hardcover edition as follows:
Vujicic, Nick.
    Stand strong : you can overcome bullying (and other stuff that keeps you down) / Nick Vujicic. — First edition.
        pages cm
    ISBN 978-0-307-73093-0 — ISBN 978-0-307-73094-7 (electronic) 1. Violence—Religious aspects—Christianity. 2. Bullying—Religious aspects. 3. Christian teenagers—Religious life. I. Title.
    BT736.15.V85 2013
    248.8'3—dc23

                                                                2013039728

Printed in the United States of America
2015—First Trade Paperback Edition

10 9 8 7 6 5 4 3 2 1

SPECIAL SALES
Most WaterBrook Multnomah books are available at special quantity discounts when purchased in bulk by corporations, organizations, and special-interest groups. Custom imprinting or excerpting can also be done to fit special needs. For information, please e-mail SpecialMarkets@WaterBrookMultnomah.com or call 1-800-603-7051.

This book, which strives to help put an end to the global bullying epidemic, is dedicated to my son, Kiyoshi, in hopes that my child and yours will grow up in a better and kinder world.

Contents

Why Me?
Why You?

You are not a
Bullying is a
epidemic.

I am a bully's dream, no doubt about it.

No arms. No legs. No defense.

Born without limbs for reasons never determined, I was blessed in so many other ways. My greatest blessing was a loving and supportive family. They sheltered and encouraged me for the first years of my life. But once I left the protective shelter of family for the hallways and playgrounds of elementary school, I felt like I had a target on my chest that said, "Bullies, aim here."

I felt alone in my fear of bullies, but I wasn't alone. And neither are you.

If you've been bullied, the first thing you need to understand is that their attacks, taunts, and mean acts aren't really about you, any flaws you might have, or anything you might have done. Bullies have their own issues. They pick on you to make themselves feel better, to vent their anger, to feel more powerful, or even because they can't think of anything else to do.

I know it's lame, but it's true.

When I was a teenager, I wasted a lot of time trying to figure out why bullies picked on me. There was one guy in particular who really got inside my head. He bullied everybody, but for some reason I took it personally. I obsessed over his motives. Finally I realized that his bullying wasn't about my problems. It was about his.

You may have a bully who has had the same impact on you, getting inside your head, knotting your stomach with stress, and tormenting your dreams because you can't figure out why you are the target. I'm here to ease your mind and lighten that burden.

Your bully's motives don't matter. You do.

Your safety and your happiness are important to me and everyone else who loves and cares about you; so instead of focusing on why a bully is picking on you, let's focus on helping you feel secure and happy again.

Does that sound like a plan? I think so!

But before we move on, I want you to know that there is no single infallible strategy for dealing one-on-one with bullies. And I certainly don't recommend you resort to violence if you can help it! Don't ever let a bully lure you into a fight. If a bully attacks you, defend yourself but get away as fast as you can. If you have any reason to think a bully is going to harm you physically, you need to talk to an adult who can help you before that happens.

THE BULLYING EPIDEMIC

It's important to understand from the beginning that many people share your pain in dealing with this problem. Being bullied, sadly, is as common as catching a cold or stubbing your toe. I travel all over the world talking to young people about this issue. No matter where I go, bullying is a major topic of concern. Teens in every school in every town and every country tell me they have mental, emotional, physical, and spiritual pain because of being bullied.

A teen in China told me that he'd tried to commit suicide eight times because of being bullied at school. A cute little Korean girl in Boise, Idaho, came up to me crying after I gave a speech on bullying. She said, "I get teased every day about being Korean because I'm the only Asian in the whole school."

I hear similar stories from bullying victims in Chile, Brazil, Australia, Russia, Serbia, and around the world. Bullying is everywhere, and it takes many forms. Most of us are familiar with childhood bullies who threaten to beat us up, make fun of us, or turn friends against us. Adults may experience bullying in the form of sexual harassment or as discrimination based on race, religion, sexual identity, or disabilities. Bullies can be your boss, coworkers, teachers, coaches, boyfriends, or girlfriends—anyone who abuses his power or position.

It's sad to say, but parents can be bullies too. Suicides are a major problem among young people in Asia, and part of the problem is that many teens are under incredible pressure to earn top grades so they can make it into the best schools and get the best jobs for the most pay. Parents naturally want their children to do well, but when a mother and father give love and support only if their child is successful in their eyes, it is a form of bullying. There was one case in which the parents burned their child with cigarettes because her grades were not up to their standards. That's an extreme case to be sure, but I've encountered similar stories around the world.

The most common bullying experience is being taunted or ridiculed for being "different" in some way. I'm the poster child for this. For most of my life, I've been a bully magnet. I've heard every imaginable nasty comment about my lack of limbs. Cruel jokes. Even physical threats.

> Still, if you are being
> bullied, it hurts.

It didn't help that my family moved a couple of times when I was in school. We went from one side of Australia to the other, then we moved to the United States and back again. At each new school, I wasn't just the only kid with no arms and no legs; I was usually the only kid in a wheelchair. When we moved to the United States, I hit the bully-target trifecta: I was the only kid in my school with no arms and no legs, the only kid in a wheelchair, *and* the only kid with an Australian accent!

Different? *Me, mate?*

Sure, I stood out from the crowd, and the fact that I was often the new kid without friends made me an even easier target. But I realized early on that bullies would find a reason to pick on anyone. They called the smart kids "nerds," the tall kids "bird legs," and the short kids "runts." If perfect people existed, bullies probably would mock them for being "too perfect."

Still, if you are being bullied, it hurts. It's a terrible experience that often seems like it will never end. As someone who endured it throughout my teenage years and still runs into it from time to time, I want to give you hope and peace. You can rise above and beyond it.

RISING ABOVE

God put you on this earth because He loves you and He has a plan for you. With His help and the guidance offered in this book, you will be able to put your bullies in their proper place so their taunts and shunning won't matter to you. My experience proves that anyone can rise above bullying and have a ridiculously wonderful life. I know you can do the same.

To help you begin, I want to plant a thought in your brain. This is blatant mind control, of course; so if you want to block it, go ahead and put tinfoil around your head. (It will look silly, but that's okay with me if it's okay with you.) The thought I want you to consider is that while being bullied is an awful thing to go through, it can also be a great opportunity.

I know what you are thinking: *Nick must have been kicked in the head by a kangaroo!* No, it was a wallaby. But aside from that, I believe you can turn your evil bully into a source for good in your life. Instead of letting your antagonist drive you nuts, depress you, dog your every thought, ruin your sleep, and stomp all over your dreams, why not turn the tables?

> While being bullied is an awful thing to go through, it can also be a great opportunity.

Bullies want to abuse you. Instead of allowing that, you can use them as your personal motivators. Power up and let the bully eat your dust. In the pages that follow, I will help you build your antibully antibodies. This is a process that works by building strength from the inside out, from your deepest thoughts and feelings—your heart and soul—to the way you see the world, make decisions, and take actions. You build your bully defense system from the inside out by

1. figuring out who you are so no bully can tell you differently or make you feel badly;

2. taking responsibility for your own behavior and happiness so bullies have no ultimate power over you;

3. establishing strong values that no bully can shake;

4. creating a safety zone within yourself where you can go mentally to draw strength and comfort;

5. building strong and supportive relationships to stand up for you against bullies;

6. learning to monitor and manage your responses to the emotions triggered by bullying;

7. developing a spiritual foundation to help you be at peace and be strong against bullying;

8. taking the opportunity to learn from your bullying experience so that you can become stronger, wiser, more confident, more faith filled, and more prepared to handle any challenges;

9. creating your bully defense strategy so you are prepared to handle bullies of all kinds; and

10. mastering empathy so you are aware of the needs of others and serve them whenever possible to help them overcome bullying.

Once all those things are in place, you will have your own bully defense system. Then you can join me in working to eradicate the epidemic of bullying so no one else has to suffer. Together, with God's help, we can bring an end to the bullying epidemic.

Too often people who are bullied become bullies themselves. It's a vicious cycle, and one of my goals in writing this book is to break it by first helping you so you can then help me and all the others around the globe dedicated to ridding the world of bullying.

We can do this. We can band together and make this a bully-free world. In 2012, I visited a school in Hawaii to talk about bullying. About a year later, the headmaster sent me a letter saying that my visit had changed the school. He said they did not have a single instance of bullying for an entire year after I talked to the students!

You are taking the first step in joining this campaign by reading this book. Please, when you are done, pass it on to others. Share what you've learned from it with your siblings, friends, parents, teachers, and anyone else you think might benefit.

If you are a teen and you are overwhelmed by bullying in any form, this book will help you understand that the game bullies play is designed to make you feel bad so they can feel superior. Refuse to play that game. Instead, believe those who love you when we say you matter to us and to your Creator. You are a child of God, created in His image. You are beautiful. You are the perfectly unique *you*.

That doesn't mean you are flawless, but that's the beauty of it. We are all perfect and imperfect at the same time. God designed us this way because there is beauty in both, and purpose too.

After reading this book, you will be able to make the following statements with confidence and clarity:

- Bullies can't hurt me or define me because I have defined myself. I know who I am and where I am going.
- I don't give anyone else the power to make me feel badly. I take responsibility for my own happiness.
- My values are unshakable. I have a plan for my life guided by them.
- My strength comes from within, and no bully can make me feel insecure.
- I know my family and friends will always stand up for me, just as I will for them.
- I am aware of my emotions, especially anger and fear, and I control my response to them so that I stay positive in my thoughts and actions.
- My spiritual life is strong and empowering. I know I was created for a purpose and I am loved unconditionally. Where I am weak, my Creator is strong.
- I find something positive to take away from every challenge, including being bullied.
- I reach out to help others at every opportunity, especially those who are being bullied in any way.

Together we will build your bully defense system. You will feel stronger than you've ever felt, and you will be better prepared to face all the challenges life might throw at you.

I love you.

Nick's Notes for Chapter One

- Bullying is a global epidemic. So if you are being bullied, you are not alone—and there is plenty of help available.

- When a bully picks on you, it isn't about you or any flaws you might have; it's about the bully's own issues. So try not to take it personally.

- There is no single infallible strategy for dealing with each and every bully. Your best bet is to work on building strength from within and strategies for every scenario you might face.

- If a bully attacks you, defend yourself but get away as fast as you can. If you have any reason to think a bully is going to harm you physically, you need to talk to an adult who can help you before that happens.

Two

Become a Bully's Nightmare

Figure out who you are so no bully can tell you differently.

The dude was drunk as a skunk. My wife and I were swimming in a resort pool on a road trip. He kept staring at me. At first I couldn't hear what he was saying because his speech was slurred, but I knew it was something bad.

As he got closer, my fears were confirmed. He pointed at my little foot as I sat on the edge of the pool. He said crude things about my foot and my body. Then he badgered me with obnoxious questions intended to embarrass and belittle me.

Mostly he made a fool of himself. He didn't need my help doing that, so I kept quiet and let him wear himself out. After a few minutes, he stumbled into the hotel. I prayed for him. I really did. I prayed for him to walk full speed into a closed glass door! (Just kidding. Maybe.)

I try to be like Jesus when it comes to dealing with bullies. He is the supreme example of someone who was bullied for His religious beliefs. Yet Jesus was so cool, so true to Himself that

He never used His power to strike back at them. I'm sure Jesus could have zapped His tormentors with a lightning bolt if He'd wanted to. Instead, He dealt with bullies just as He dealt with all people—with compassion from a foundation of love and redemption.

I wasn't usually that strong. My experiences with bullies often left me feeling both intimidated and angry, not to mention depressed, anxious, stressed, and sick to my stomach.

As an adult, I'm better equipped to rise above bullying. But I admit that the bully at the resort pool did bother me. He made me uncomfortable just as he made everyone else around the pool uncomfortable with his drunken rant.

Did he make me ashamed or insecure or depressed? Not at all! You see, I now have the best defense anyone can have when it comes to bullies, one that I will share with you in this book. Our first step in building your own bully defense system is to help you define yourself so that no bully and no other person can tell you who you are.

A SENSE OF SELF

This is a lesson I learned the hard way. I let the taunts of bullies stick to me like burs when I was a kid. I pretended to be sick so I could stay home from school and avoid them.

When I went to school, I hid in the bushes so they couldn't

find me. I was very vulnerable, and bullies took advantage of that. There were so many questions that I couldn't answer, including this big one: *If God loves all of His children, why did He create me with so many imperfections?*

Most kids my age were worried that their noses were too big or that their zits would never go away. I'd lie in bed at night tortured by thoughts about what I lacked: *Couldn't He have given me at least arms, or at least legs, or at least one arm or one leg? Why would He leave me with no limbs at all? What purpose does that serve? What purpose can I serve? How can I function in a world designed for people with limbs?*

My nagging doubts about my value and my future were only made worse by bullies who said mean things to me, made jokes about me, or shunned me like I wasn't a real person. All of this weighed so heavily on my mind that I had suicidal thoughts. A few times I had urges to throw myself off ledges or countertops.

Finally, around the age of ten, I did make an attempt to drown myself in the bathtub. I put my head underwater and held my breath for a long time, but I couldn't do it. I had visions of my parents and my brother and sister crying at my funeral. I couldn't stand the thought of them grieving or feeling hurt or guilty. It wasn't their fault; how could I cause them such pain?

That day, I decided suicide was not an option. The self-destructive feelings still came, but over time they diminished.

Still, I know firsthand that bullies can drive you to despair. I understand those feelings.

If you've felt depressed and had thoughts of hurting or killing yourself, please do not allow bullies to take your joy and your will to live from you. Why give anyone that power? Don't let them take you away from the wonderful life that God has in store for you.

A Better Life Awaits

If I had let bullying drive me to suicide, I would have missed a life that has been full of joy and love in measures that I never could have imagined. I would have missed marrying the love of my life, not to mention the birth of our son! I never would have had the opportunity to meet and encourage people around the world.

You and I just don't know what wonderful things are possible for our lives. Only our Creator knows what is in store for us. You may be in the dumps right now. Maybe a bully is making your life miserable. It's a horrible feeling, I know. But I can help you. You can get past this. Better days are ahead, and you don't want to miss them, do you?

We all have challenges. Yours may be far greater than mine. I was born without limbs, but I was blessed in many other ways. I believe we all have the power to overcome challenges through determination and God's help. Remember, you may feel you don't have the strength to handle a challenge, but He does.

I lack limbs, but I've hung in there and come through some major storms. I've dealt with bullies all my life. In fact, I'm still dealing with bullies—and I'm a married man with a child. I've learned to handle the bullies, mostly by controlling how I respond to them and by building a solid foundation from which to fend them off.

You can learn to do the same. By sharing my experiences, I'd like to give you a *hand* with that. (A sense of humor helps too!) For a time in my teen years, I thought I would never be able to go to college, to earn a living, or to make a contribution to this world. I thought no woman could ever love me as a husband, and I never thought I would be able to be a father and hold my child to my heart.

I was wrong, wrong, wrong, and wrong again! The bullies who said nasty things to me had it wrong, and so did I. My life—the same life that looked so dark for a while because of bullying and insecurities—has been absolutely and ridiculously wonderful!

I never could have imagined what God had in store for a guy born without arms or legs. You can't imagine what your Creator's plan for you is either. I suggest that we both stick around to see the good that life has in store for us.

Turning a Negative into a Positive

Maybe a bully has teased you about being short, tall, skinny, or different in some way. I've learned that the things that make us feel different can be our greatest assets. I know that being criticized or shunned is painful. Yet having experienced that pain can also make you a more compassionate, empathetic, understanding, and thankful person.

You've probably heard the saying—or even the song by Kelly Clarkson—that says, "What doesn't kill you makes you stronger." On my bad days, I'd think, *Sure, but it still hurts right now!* That's true too. But you can use a bully's taunts as motivation to grow wiser, stronger, smarter, and more confident than ever before.

> "What doesn't kill you
> makes you stronger."

If someone hurt you, then become the person who reaches out to others who are hurting. If you were not treated with compassion, then change that pattern by offering compassion to others. If no one stood up for you, then stand up for someone else. My message is simple: if a man with no arms or legs can overcome challenges like bullying, anyone can. I gave my imperfect self with all my broken pieces a chance, and look what happened!

You see, what happens in our lives isn't about chance. It's about choice. You and I may not be able to stop bullies and thoughtless people from saying and doing hurtful things, but we do have the ultimate power—the power to choose how we respond and how we live.

You Are Stronger than You Think

Bullies look for people they can overpower with words, with their fists, or by isolating and manipulating them in person or online. They look for weaknesses, sensitivities, or insecurities they can exploit. You probably have all of the above, right? Who doesn't?

Everyone has something to be insecure or sensitive about. That doesn't make us weak. It makes us human, but also a little vulnerable, which again isn't unusual at all. Being vulnerable can make us more sympathetic and thoughtful in our dealings with others. You can be vulnerable and still be strong.

Bullies also prey on people they can isolate, which can include the new kid in a school or neighborhood or a teen on the Internet at home. I'll offer more on this later in the book, but keep in mind that isolating yourself from other people over long periods is not a good thing. I've been there.

When you don't have someone you can talk to, negative thoughts creep in. Even little things that normally wouldn't bug you can get to you. Bullies love that. They are like hurricanes. They swoop in and tear away at anything that isn't solid, well grounded, and tethered to strong supports. But we're going to make you bully proof by building a strong foundation that never cracks.

This isn't about being cocky. It's about being so secure and strong that no bully will ever be able to make you feel weak or worthless or unworthy. You will know exactly who you are and what value you offer the world.

This doesn't mean bullies won't come after you. Some of them like a challenge. But trying to bully you will be like beating their heads against a wall. Your self-confidence will drive them crazy, and eventually they'll go looking for a weaker target; or, even better, they'll decide that bullying is just a bad deal and give it up!

Faking It to Make It

What we're looking at here is not a new thing for teens. I think most psychologists and psychiatrists agree that the teen years are when most of us begin to forge our identities, figuring out who we are, where we fit in, and what we can build our lives around. When I was entering my teen years, I wanted so badly to fit in with all the other guys. I didn't want anyone to perceive me as weak or insecure, so guess what I did? I pretended to be someone else. *Not a good move, Nick!*

I tried to fit in by acting tough and swearing like the guys I was trying to impress. This was very strange behavior for me. I can't remember ever even hearing a cussword until I reached high school. There was certainly no swearing in my home.

My parents raised us to love God and to honor Him at all times. Our lives were built around our faith. My brother and sister and I were very sheltered from the world in some ways; we weren't even allowed to listen to any radio unless it was a Christian station.

God must have been very disappointed when He heard me swearing, but I'm sure He understood that I was a little lost. My first weeks of high school were eyeopening. Everyone cursed! At least it seemed like that. There were so many swearwords flying around I began to wonder if I had it wrong and maybe the words that I thought were bad really weren't. It was like I had discovered a whole new language.

Seriously, I became convinced that swearing was just the normal way teens talked. I desperately wanted to seem normal and cool and like a rugged guy, so I abandoned the real Nick and became Foulmouthed Nick.

I started swearing because I was scared of not fitting in. There is nothing wrong with wanting to fit in and be accepted, but there is something wrong with abandoning your values and beliefs to do it.

> Be so comfortable with yourself that other people feel comfortable with you too.

I was rejecting myself in hopes that no one else would reject me. Crazy, isn't it? We all make adjustments to get along with other people. We all have to accommodate the wants and needs of those around us to some degree. That's all part of living in a larger world—being part of a family, a community, a nation, and the world.

But you should never do things you feel are wrong because you want to fit in. You don't need to pretend to be someone else to fit in. You already have a place on this earth.

Try this instead: Be so comfortable with yourself that other people feel comfortable with you too. Create a life that makes you so joyful that they will want to share in your happiness.

WEARING A MASK

For a while, I played a dumb game and tried to act like the "cool kids." I have no idea why cursing was considered cool, but

I fell into the habit quickly. It was like we had our own language, so maybe it made us feel independent and grown up.

I felt guilty, too, because every time I swore, I was defying the standards set by my parents. I had no reason to defy my parents. They loved me and wanted only the best for me. I always knew that.

Maybe I was subconsciously declaring my independence from them. Those little rebellions are part of growing up too, though probably not the part that most parents enjoy.

As kids we are told what to do and when to do it, so the teen years seem to be the season when we declare our independence a bit, or a lot. Teens are expected to do that to some degree. The problem is that we aren't independent yet. We still live at home. We still depend on our parents to pay for our food, clothing, and shelter, so they feel we should live by their rules.

It's an age-old battle, but it can be more like a gentle tug of war than a nuclear war if you keep things in perspective and try to understand each other rather than simply react emotionally. I was lucky to have parents who always had my best interests at heart, even when we disagreed. My parents were also very protective. I couldn't blame them for that, but I was much more comfortable taking risks.

When I first started cursing to be more like my friends, I felt uncomfortable. I knew it wasn't me. Half the time, I'd be asking myself, *What are you doing talking like this? What's your problem?* Then the other half—my Bad Nick side—would say, *I'm just being cool like everyone else. It's just an act. I'm playing a role to fit in.*

I was giving myself positive feedback for negative actions. I was creating a false face, a mask. I ignored the Good Nick voice telling me I wasn't being authentic. I ignored it because I just wanted to get through the day without being bullied or made to feel like a "handicapped" kid or anything other than a normal guy.

SMOKE AND MIRRORS

The longer you pretend to be someone you aren't, the harder it is to go back to the real you. When I stopped being true to myself, it created all sorts of problems with my relationships, my performance in school, and my self-esteem.

> The longer you pretend to be someone you aren't, the harder it is to go back to the real you.

I had to confront some tough questions eventually. One of these was, *How can I be honest with myself when I lie to everyone else?* After a while I didn't want to pretend anymore. I looked inside and asked, *How far am I willing to go? How long can I keep this up? What will my parents think of my acting like this? Who do I really want to please—those who love me or those who just want to control me for their own purposes?*

By cursing, I put out a false image. In my heart, I still felt I was a good Christian kid, but my actions weren't consistent with being a good Christian kid—and people judged me not by what was in my heart but by the way I acted.

Never Too Cool for Christ

For a while, my actions were not consistent with my faith—or my beliefs. Cursing wasn't the only bit of phoniness I put out there. For a time, I turned my back on my fellow believers. The serious Christian kids at our school had a Friday lunchtime prayer group. Only a handful of kids participated, and they took some teasing and bullying over it. Some called them Holy Rollers and Jesus Freaks.

I thought they were really nice, genuine people of faith, but I didn't join their Friday prayer group. When someone asked me why I didn't go with them, I said I'd rather be with my non-Christian friends. I felt uncomfortable saying that, and it bothered me for a long time. There was a reason for that feeling of unease. Again, I wasn't being true to my values, my beliefs, and my true self. Part of this was because I was trying to fit in and I wasn't yet comfortable with acting like a Christian. I didn't want to be called a Holy Roller or a Jesus Freak. I was afraid it might pigeonhole me and the non-Christian kids wouldn't want to hang out with me anymore.

You can get away with being inauthentic for a time, but you really can't fake it to make it long term. Sooner or later, living a lie will come back to haunt you. There will be a price to pay. In my case, one of those days of reckoning came when I accidentally took Foulmouthed Nick home.

I let one cussword fly, and my mom was all over it.

"What was that you said, Nick?"

"Oops, I'm sorry. I'm sorry. I don't know where that came from!"

Cursing was so uncharacteristic of me that I think my mom wasn't sure what to do about it. She was stunned. I think she made me promise never to do it again, and after a few other chastisements, she let it slide. Still, that slip-up made me realize once again that I wasn't living my faith.

Slips of the Tongue

I considered myself a good Christian who'd given his life to Christ, but the part of my brain that regulated speech apparently didn't get the memo.

As much as I tried to eliminate swearwords from my

vocabulary, they kept popping up. I managed to control myself at home for the most part, but when I was in school, surrounded by teens dropping the f-bomb right and left, I struggled to keep my conversations PG. Slowly, I cleaned up my act. My friends Scott and Reese noticed the change in my vocabulary and asked me about it.

"I don't want to swear anymore," I said.

"Why not? What's wrong with it?"

"I was brought up to live as a Christian. Swearing isn't part of a godly life," I explained. "God doesn't like swearing."

Scott and Reese were good friends. They may not have understood or agreed, but they immediately tried to find ways to help me swear off swearing.

"I have an idea," Scott said. "Instead of using the f-word, you can say 'fruitcake'!"

That seemed like a crazy idea at first, but research has shown that shouting words that end in a hard consonant sound triggers chemicals in the brain that provide some emotional and physical release. So, as silly as it seemed, I tried using "fruitcake" as a swearword substitute.

It didn't work for me. It just made me think of bad holiday desserts, and it was too long. By the time I got through the *fruit* and to the *cake,* something was lost. Scott then suggested I try "fire truck" instead, but I decided to go cold turkey on the cursing.

But swearing off swearing proved to be more difficult than I'd imagined. Cursing had become a serious habit. I kept slipping up and letting the profanities fly, but gradually I learned to shut down the potty-mouth machine. Around the age of sixteen, I went for eleven months and three weeks without swearing. Yes, I counted the days. I was desperate to break the Nasty Nick mold, but then I had a particularly bad relapse one day when something set off my temper.

I took God's name in vain, which stunned everyone within earshot, including me. I can't remember what it was that made me slip up after holding my tongue so long, but I felt horrible, just horrible. So I asked for His help. I surrendered to God, praying for an end to my swearing habit.

If you ever question whether He is a forgiving God, read 1 John 1:9 ("If we confess our sins, he is faithful and just and will forgive us our sins and purify us from all unrighteousness") and remember this: after I confessed and asked for His mercy, the good Lord wiped my vocabulary clean. I was very grateful, and I did everything possible to stay away from others who cursed.

I decided the "cool kids" were not so cool for me and returned to my circle of Christian friends. They forgave me my trespasses and welcomed me back into the fold. In their company I no longer felt like an impostor. It felt natural, and I took no offense from there on out if somebody teased me for being a Holy Roller.

Once again, as the Doobie Brothers song says, Jesus was all right with me. (I just hope I was all right with Him!)

Something strange and wonderful happened when I stepped into a place where I felt very comfortable and accepted: suddenly, it seemed like *everyone* wanted to be my friend! Even most of the bullies backed off. Once I finally stopped trying to hide who I really was and just put it out there that I was a Christian kid, people in general were more accepting of me, kinder to me, and even eager to get to know me. I'm thankful for the good and true friends who loved me and were always there for me. I could be myself around them, and as they saw me mature, we grew closer together, which helped me deal with the bullies.

BEING THE TRUE YOU

I realized then that one of the greatest blessings in life is to be honest *about* yourself and *with* yourself. Once I found a group of kids who loved me just as I was—Bible-loving, armless, legless me—my confidence soared, and that seemed to act as a magnet to attract other people.

It was my mistake to think I had to transform myself to be cool. Teens are hard on themselves, and they can be hard on others too. As teens, we tend to put people in boxes instead of just letting them show us who they are. We all have many interests, traits, and moods. You shouldn't put anyone in a box, least of all yourself.

Once I decided that pleasing God was more important than being the popular guy, I felt at peace. I also became less judgmental and more accepting of others after I realized that I didn't have to fake it to make it. Being secure and comfortable in your identity, trusting that you have value, and having a strong sense of your purpose are important in every aspect of life. Those qualities also help make you less vulnerable to bullying.

How do you build a strong and secure identity, self-worth, and sense of purpose? Nearly all teenagers hit a point when they have a sort of identity crisis, wondering what their roles are in life, where they fit in, and what they have to contribute. If you've experienced this, don't worry. It's one of those universal human experiences. If you haven't felt that way yet, you will sooner or later. We all are different, and we all have our own timetables.

THE ANSWERS WITHIN YOU

You may be asking yourself the questions we all ask eventually when trying to determine our places in the world. That's good; it shows you are growing up and preparing for the next big stages of life. But where are the answers to be found?

Let me assure you, every answer you need is somewhere inside of you. Don't panic if you can't figure out each and every one right away. Some are meant to unfold and present themselves over time. The main thing right now is to know that you don't have to rely on anyone else to tell you who you are or what your value is. God put you here for a purpose. He gave you a unique package of features that includes your physical appearance, your talents, your brainpower, and other components that make you beautiful and special.

> Let me assure you, every answer you need is somewhere inside of you.

We all have strengths and weaknesses, of course. Some of us may even be missing a few bits and pieces here and there. My advice to you is to build your strengths. That way, when a bully picks on your weaknesses, it won't matter!

If you believe in your own value, no bully can take it away from you. If you know in your heart that God loves you and that you were created for His purpose, no bully can tell you otherwise.

We all have times when we feel down. We all screw up. We all fall flat on our faces from time to time. Insecurities can dog you. When I was a teenager, I'd sometimes get these huge bright red pimples on my nose. There I was, no arms and legs, but I had zits! Some of the pimples on my nose were so big they seemed to block my vision. At times like that, I'd look in the mirror and struggle to keep it together. One thing that helped was to force myself to name one good physical feature I possessed and then focus on it.

"I have nice eyes," I'd say. "People always tell me I have nice eyes, so I'm going with that."

Why can't we do that for ourselves? If we let bullies drag us down with their cruelty and meanness, why can't we pull ourselves back up by being friends to ourselves and building up our confidence and spirits when we need a boost? (My big fear was that the next day someone would tell me that I had bags under my eyes—ruining the one good thing I thought I had going!)

Teens are often very critical of themselves. In those years, we're always comparing ourselves to classmates or friends and asking why we can't be tall like him or pretty like her or more popular or more athletic or smarter. If we can be critical of ourselves, why can't we encourage ourselves too?

There were times in high school when I seemed to take one hit, one snub, one cruel comment after another. I'd be dragging around with my head down, feeling sorry for poor, poor Nick. Then a classmate would walk by and say, "Nick, you're looking good today!" Or, "Nick, that speech you gave in class was wonderful!"

A single kind word or a little bit of encouragement would

change my whole attitude! For weeks, I'd hang on to those positive words and use them to keep myself out of the doldrums. It's a little crazy that we can allow one mean or cruel or nasty comment to send us into despair or depression. Why not focus on the good stuff, the kind words, and the gifts we've been given instead?

So here's my suggestion for a simple, easy-to-apply, no muss, no fuss first step to building your antibully 1.0 operating system. Be a friend to yourself. Forgive your mistakes, your flaws, and your failures. Be kind to yourself instead. Focus on the good.

> Be a friend to yourself.
> Forgive your mistakes,
> your flaws, and your failures.

What have you got to lose? There is so much to be gained by this attitude of self-acceptance and self-love. You will be braver, more resilient, harder to hurt, happier, more positive, and more likable. To begin this process, write down some of your strengths and successes on a separate sheet of paper. Make a list of those things that you do well or things that people have complimented you on. Include things you've accomplished, problems you've solved on your own, repair jobs you've done, good decisions you've made, cool things you've created, goals you've reached, risks that have worked out, and people or even animals you've helped.

BE THE MIRACLE

One of my guiding philosophies is that if you can't get a miracle for yourself, be one for someone else. When I was feeling bummed out as a teen, it really helped lift my spirits if I just stepped away from my problems for a while and offered to help other people with theirs. I've benefited so much by trying to be of benefit to others. It's made me so much stronger—strong enough to handle anything negative or hurtful that comes my way.

A California teen named Michael wrote to my Life Without Limbs website to share his own story about the blessings that come from being a blessing to others. Here is what he wrote:

> I was born premature with a crooked feet [*sic*] and a bad lung where I couldn't breathe well but had surgery on it and on my right eye 10 times but thank God I am still here today.... I'm trying to be the best I can be—I am going to Los Medanos College to become a special ed aid one day to help special needs kids. That's what I really would love to do. People made fun of me a lot

growing up. I used to do all kinds of bad stuff and try to get my security from people to run away from my problems. I have learned to forgive people and not let them get me down and also not be controlled by the things I used to be enslaved by. I studied the Bible with my church friends and learned a lot about God, myself and my life. On April 4, 2010 during Easter I was inspired to get baptized and live a new life for God.

If you are having a tough time dealing with a bully or someone who tears you down—or if you have difficulty understanding and appreciating your own value—try volunteering to help at a local charity, a facility for the disabled, a veterans' hospital, or a homeless shelter. Ask some adults in your life, such as a teacher, a school administrator, or your minister, if they know of a place where you could make a difference. I promise you will be grateful for the experience. It's likely you will come to feel better about yourself, and that will make you stronger emotionally too.

If you feel like you haven't done enough with your life so far, set some reasonable goals and go after them step by step until you achieve them. Then celebrate that accomplishment. Reward yourself. Feel good about what you've done, and then set the bar a little higher and go after another goal.

Once you've built up your self-confidence and expertise,

don't be afraid to set the bar higher and higher. I've done that for most of my life. Sometimes I've fallen flat on my face, quite literally. You won't always succeed either, but as long as you keep stretching and reaching higher, you will create opportunities to succeed. The immediate goal is to make you bully proof, but your ability to deal with setbacks and challenges of any kind will only improve as you grow in self-confidence and self-love.

Nick's Notes for Chapter Two

- Once you know who you are and feel secure about yourself, no bully can make you feel insecure or steal your joy.
- You were created for a purpose, and that means you have value and a future of unlimited potential that you don't want to miss.
- You grow stronger and more bully proof when you accept and love yourself, even as you work every day on being the best person you can possibly be.

Three

Owning It

Take responsibility for
your own life so bullies
have no power over you.

Back in my early teen years I let bullies get to me in a big way. I allowed them to hurt me and make me feel worthless. I felt sorry for myself. My uncle John picked up on that and put a stop to my pity party then and there.

"Nick, no one can ever change who you are," he said. "You can cut out someone's tongue, pluck out his eyes, and plug his ears so he can't taste, see, or hear, but that still doesn't change who that person is inside. No one can touch your spirit or your soul."

Thanks, Uncle John. I needed that!

My uncle was telling me to take responsibility for my own happiness and my own self-esteem. I couldn't stop bullies from picking on me. Most of the time you can't either. But you can control whether you let them get to you by stepping up and deciding that no one can make you feel badly about yourself if you don't let them.

I encourage you to keep this phrase in your mind when

faced with bullying: *You can say terrible things to me, but you can't touch who I am inside. You can't make me feel badly about myself. I know who I am, and I stand on my own.*

Do-It-Yourself Happiness

You should consider your life a do-it-yourself project when it comes to creating your own happiness and self-esteem. Take responsibility for being the best person you can become. Make the most of your talents. Build on your strengths, and work on your weaknesses. Be humble, but love yourself, while always doing your best to develop your talents and pursue your purpose. When you generate that kind of positive energy, you attract supporters and discourage bullies from picking on you.

Self-love and self-confidence come to you when you accept responsibility for your own happiness and success. I learned this as a child, but I had to remind myself of it time and again as challenges came my way. You may need to do the same. Think of yourself as your own coach in that regard. Remind yourself of past victories, and use them to build strength when faced with bullies and other challenges. Be grateful for the ability to control your responses to whatever life throws at you. It's like a superpower that allows you to turn even bad things into learning experiences that can benefit you later in life.

One thing I did not lack as a child was determination, and

my parents and siblings quickly decided the best option in most cases was to "let Nick do it for himself." They did not coddle me, which I appreciate very much—at least now. There were times as a kid when I might have yearned to be spoiled rotten and treated like a prince, but my family made sure that didn't happen. They didn't cut me any slack because I lacked limbs.

Even today, my parents are always supportive and encouraging, but they never allow me to wallow in self-pity or to hide from my responsibilities. As a boy, I did chores around the house just like my brother and sister. I had to make my bed, clean my room, and run the vacuum cleaner! If I complained about it being harder for someone without arms or legs—and believe me, I did—my parents told me to figure it out. Theirs wasn't exactly tough love, but they wanted me to be able to handle everything the world might throw at me.

My family, including all my cousins, treated me like a normal kid. They teased me and made jokes at my expense, but always with love and affection. I didn't always understand why my parents expected me to do everything on my own, but now I do, and I'm grateful for it. They had a son who lacked legs, but they wanted me to stand on my own.

As I got older, I wanted to do that desperately. I hated the thought of being dependent on other people, and I took pride in figuring out how to do things on my own. My parents encouraged that, and they helped devise ways for me to turn on lights, brush my teeth, comb my hair, and do other tasks without limbs.

Those small victories over my disabilities gave me strength for bigger challenges later in life—but I had to learn to tap into them to build my confidence. There are a lot of things you can't control when you are young. Most teens depend on their parents for food, clothing, shelter, transportation, and spending money. You are not financially independent. You can't move into a penthouse apartment or beachfront condo. Yet even when you become financially independent as an adult, many things are still beyond your control.

We can choose to take responsibility for our own happiness and our responses to being bullied.

The good news is that while you can't control certain things that happen to you—like bullies, storms, illness, or challenges at home—you can choose whether you respond in a negative or positive manner. No matter where I am speaking in the world, whether it's central California, South America, or China, young people ask me how I can be so joyful when I have such severe physical disabilities. I tell them it's because I choose to focus instead on all the good things in my life.

I have a choice. You have a choice. We can choose to give in to self-pity or victimhood when bullies pick on us, or we can choose to take responsibility for our own happiness and our responses to being bullied. Teens may not have as much control over their lives as adults, but it's a powerful thing to take control of your actions, especially your responses to life's challenges.

When you think of being bullied, it's usually in terms of another person who is taunting you, pushing you around, or ostracizing you socially. But there are many other forms of bullying, including religious persecution, dictatorships, sex slavery, and physical and sexual abuse. Even illnesses and disabilities can be bullies in a sense because they restrict your freedom and try to limit your life. Melissa wrote about this in an inspiring e-mail she sent to me:

> I am from a little town in England. I have two very rare conditions—Dystonia [a neurological movement disorder] and Chronic Regional Pain Syndrome. It started with a hairline fracture in my ankle and now I am wheelchair bound. I cannot walk at all, and there is a 90% chance I will lose my right leg from the knee down. The Dystonia is a neurological condition that we didn't know I had until I broke my ankle, it was underlying and once that was set off, the CRPS started to affect me. I was asked to leave college because I wanted to do physiotherapy. I ended up doing physio every week…for 15 months,

and twice a day for 30 minutes every day at home. Turns out that physio would never help me, and I'm currently seeing the "top" doctors to see if my hips and left leg can be saved. Anyway, once I realized that this condition was for life, I made the decision that I wanted to help others, I wanted to inspire others, just like Nick. And I know that Nick believes in God (I don't, but I'm open minded and respect that opinion), but I believe in Nick and how he inspires me. I've started teaching myself psychology, and then I'll teach myself other subjects. I've made my own website about my conditions and it offers advice, and I have a blog as well. Many people tell me that I inspire them already, but I want to do more—I want to inspire people just like Nick. I also have a "journal," so I can look back at it later on in life and reflect, or use it to help me help others. I'm not an inspiration yet, but, hopefully, one day, I can help others, I can make my mum proud, and eventually be an inspiration, because that's what I want—I want someone to say to me "Because of you, I didn't give up on my dreams."

Isn't that precious? I would correct only one thing Melissa wrote in that letter: she is an inspiration. Her story makes me want to be an even better person, so that makes her a life changer too!

The Power of Choice

Melissa chose to take responsibility for her own happiness and her own life. She is a very wise and mature young woman. I wish I'd had her wisdom when I first began dealing with bullies in my school years. If a bully said something hurtful, I let it hurt me. If he called me a freak, I saw myself as a freak. If a bully told me that no girl would ever like me, I believed it.

I wasn't strong. I didn't take responsibility for my own happiness or self-esteem. I just didn't get it at that point, and as a result, I fell into despair and had suicidal thoughts that eventually prompted some very unwise actions. I tried to commit suicide once because bullies had convinced me there was no hope. Another time I let a bully goad me into a fight on the playground.

I wised up in high school. Bullies and cruel people still hurt my feelings and made me angry. I couldn't help that. But eventually, I learned to control my responses to bullies. Instead of lashing out or fleeing in tears, I assessed the situation with more thought. I tried to understand where each bully was coming from. Sometimes that was impossible. You can't always read a bully's motivations. Some of them are deeply troubled or just plain mean.

Please, don't ever let a bully "make" you do anything. Take responsibility and take charge. Respond to the bully in whatever way serves you best—don't take the bait, whatever it may be.

When I was in elementary school, I took the bait hook, line, and sinker. The bullies got their hooks in me, and it tore into my soul. Don't make that mistake, because it will tear you up too—and that's just what the bully wants.

I nearly took my own life after being hooked by the lie that I was a worthless freak with no future. Lies can kill you, but only if you let them into your heart. Don't let them in. Welcome the truth instead, the truth that you were perfectly created by God and delivered to this earth to serve Him and His purpose.

You are loved, and you have no idea what He has in store. Your value is not determined by anything related to your appearance. It's all about what resides inside your heart and soul.

I didn't feel like I had much power when I was a kid. To me, adults had power and kids didn't. Teachers had power. But God had power on standby for my use. I never thought that I had it, but it was there. I'd just never claimed it.

Here are suggestions that can help you unleash your own power of choice.

Step 1: Get in the Driver's Seat

When I tell you to get in the driver's seat, I mean this metaphorically of course. You may not be old enough to drive yet, but even if you are, this step isn't about driving a car; it's about accepting the responsibility to be the driving force in your own life. If you want to be happy and successful—whatever your definition of success might be—you have to tap the power within you to create the life you want, no matter what happens to you. This is a really cool concept. It's sort of like a secret power that keeps you on track and feeling good about yourself regardless of what life throws at you.

David, from Portugal, was born with spina bifida and wrote to tell me that when he was younger, he was depressed because people treated him cruelly, as if he was of less value than others. For a time, he thought about giving up, but then he decided to take control of his own life and not let bullies determine how he felt. David decided to fight for his dreams and to stay positive no matter what challenges he faced, and it changed his life.

"I usually keep a smile on my face, and it makes me happy that people like you, Nick, keep a smile too," David wrote. "I have no complaining for what I became. I fought a lot, I went down, I came up. I never gave up. Death nearly caught me twice, but here I am. All I want is that people never give up on their smiles. That's why I try my best to help others. I made mistakes, and I regret that. But I will fight every day to get better."

There is no guarantee bullies won't come after you or that every day will be a walk in the sunshine, but as long as you refuse to let anyone else take control of your feelings about yourself or your dreams and goals, you should be okay.

Step 2: Decide Where You Are Going and Stay on the Road

When you are behind the wheel, you take responsibility for getting where you want to go. So if you want a better life or the best possible life, then you'll have to prepare yourself to claim it by staying on the right road and doing all you can to avoid getting lost along the way.

You must be willing to work for what you want. You can't allow yourself to settle for something less; so make sure you set realistic goals and expectations and then commit to achieving them. The cool part is that when you take the wheel with a destination in mind and a commitment to making it, the journey becomes much more enjoyable and it becomes more difficult for anyone—including bullies—to knock you off the road.

Step 3: Fuel Up

Fueling up is about figuring out what gets your motor running, what energizes you, what drives you, and what keeps you going even when the road gets rough or you just want to pull over and take a nap. Most cars run on leaded, unleaded, or diesel fuel. Some newer cars are powered by batteries or a combination of both batteries and fuel.

People have a much wider selection of power sources. We are all driven to some degree by the need to make money, but for some people it's all about making as much money as possible. I don't think that's the greatest driving force, but it's important to know if that's what fuels you. Instead, I recommend being driven by faith, to make a difference in the world, to use your talents and gifts in service to God and His people.

Some driving forces are better than others. Some can take you to a dead end quickly; others can fulfill you and make the world a better place for everyone. If your driving force is just to make money, I'm not sure you'll ever find happiness. But if your driving force is to use your gifts in service to others, there's a good chance that you'll always have what you need. I know this because there have been many times when I had very little money, but because I was traveling the world encouraging other people and leading them to God, I felt like I had all I needed and wanted.

Step 4: Get in Gear and Put the Pedal to the Metal

I don't know about you, but when I was a teenager, I spent a lot of time sitting around with my friends and having conversations like this:

"What do you want to do?"

"I don't know. What do you want to do?"

"Wanna go see a movie?"

"I don't know; do you?"

"I don't know; do *you*?"

We would go on like that for hours and hours, never

leaving the couch because we couldn't decide what to decide. We couldn't get it in gear, and as a result, we often blew entire days doing nothing, experiencing nothing, accomplishing nothing.

That is not how you want to spend your life, is it? Then you have to put it in gear and step on the gas. You can't sit around and wait for someone else to decide what you should do. You have to make a decision, and more importantly, you have to *act* on it.

That's what Nike is talking about when its advertisements say, "Just do it!" If you need a little higher source, consider the Bible, which says that having faith means nothing unless you act on it. Yes, actions really do speak louder than words. It's good to have dreams, but you'll never claim the life you want until you get out of bed and go after them.

How does this help you deal with bullies? Well, what's easier to hit, a sitting duck or a rabbit on the run? If bullies are looking for someone to hit, their last choice will be a moving target, someone who has it in gear with the pedal to the metal on the road to a better life.

Step 5: Check the Mirror and the GPS

When I was young and dealing with bullies on a regular basis, I noticed that once I began to feel better about myself, bullies had a lot less power over me. I felt better about myself when I stuck to my beliefs and acted accordingly. I stopped cursing. I didn't pretend to be a tough guy. I talked openly about my faith. When I looked in the mirror, I saw a guy who was doing all he could to be the best Nick he could be.

> Once I began to feel better about myself, bullies had a lot less power over me.

That's what I want for you, except for the Nick part of course. I want you to be able to look in the mirror every day and feel like you are doing your best to honor your gifts and bless-ings. I don't expect you to be perfect. We all have ups and downs. Sometimes we get off track. That's okay as long as you take the time to look in the mirror and admit that you can do better and be better. You can cut yourself some slack, but be honest with yourself too. Look in the mirror and ask yourself if you've picked up some bad habits or if you are hanging out with people who don't bring out the best in you.

You should also check your personal GPS on a regular basis to make sure you are on track to becoming the person you want to be and creating the life you want to live. Sometimes you may have to take a detour. You may get lost for a while and have to find your way back. To stay on track, you'll need to check every now and then to see if where you're headed is the right direction for you. The worst thing you could do is just wander aimlessly or follow someone whose goals and dreams are different than yours.

The mirror doesn't lie. Neither does your personal GPS. If you find yourself making excuses, acting sketchy, or doing self-destructive things, then you'll know it's time to find your way back to the right road.

God cared enough to breathe life into you and put you on this earth. You need to take care of His creation and honor that precious gift.

Nick's Notes for Chapter Three

- Self-love and self-confidence come to you when you accept responsibility for your own happiness and success.

- You have the power to choose a positive response even when you encounter negative feelings and experiences like bullying. It's like a superpower, so use it to make yourself bully proof!

Four

Choose Your Path

Set a course based
on strong values that
no bully can shake.

My grandparents experienced one of the most extreme forms of bullying in their native country of Yugoslavia. During World War II, they were persecuted for their Christian faith by the Communist regime. Hundreds of thousands of their fellow Serbians were murdered, expelled, or imprisoned. My grandparents and other Christians had to conduct religious services in secret and under guard because they feared being arrested or killed for their faith.

After years of persecution, they fled their native land and moved to Australia, which is where my parents grew up, met, married, and brought me and my brother and sister into the world. You could say that bullying has had a huge impact on my family's history and my life.

It may seem strange, but in some ways, bullying has made me stronger. When things were really bad, I drew strength from the fact that my grandparents continued to practice their faith and hold true to their values even under the threat of death.

I felt that if they could show that sort of strength, so could I. When bullied as a teenager, it helped me to think about how much worse it must have been for my grandparents back in Yugoslavia. They survived and went on to better lives, which gave me hope during the tough times when bullies would make fun of me, taunt me, or shun me because I looked so much different than other kids.

The Fruit of the Spirit

My grandparents followed the example of Jesus, who was also bullied by those who hated Him for His teachings. He taught the key Christian values and He lived them, which gave Him the strength to face death and atone for our sins so that we can one day find eternal peace in heaven.

In the same way, strong values can give you the strength to deal with bullying and other challenges throughout your life. The values I'm referring to are taught in the Bible, but often other faiths promote the same or similar values. They are qualities or characteristics or feelings that bring people together, create bonds of mutual understanding and support, and benefit the greater good rather than just the individual, although over the long term each one of us benefits from them as well.

Christian values are the opposite of worldly or earthly values that are more about short-term gain for the individual, not for the greater good. Worldly values tell us to seek wealth, power, pleasure, revenge, fame, and status. Now, it's also true that good Christian people can be successful, have enjoyable lives, and be well known and admired, but those worldly things shouldn't be the goal, even if they are part of the reward.

What are the Christian values that can help you? We are told in the Bible in Galatians 5:22–23 that "the fruit of the Spirit" is love, joy, peace, patience, kindness, goodness (which includes generosity), faithfulness, gentleness, and self-control. That seems like a good list, so let's take a look at each of them and how they apply to you, your bully proofing, and the rest of your life.

The Fruit of Love

Life is too short to follow any path other than God's way. I believe heaven is real, and I want to go there as His good and faithful servant. I also want to take as many people with me as possible. I try to do that by demonstrating and expressing God's love for them whenever possible.

It is so easy and so simple to tell people they are loved, yet I am always amazed at the powerful impact it has on them. In my school presentations, I've had big, tough school bullies break down in tears and thank me when I've told them that God loves them. More than once, I've had teens tell me that no one else has ever expressed love for them.

That is so sad, especially since Jesus told us that the greatest commandment is "Love the Lord your God with all your heart and with all your soul and with all your mind," while the second greatest commandment is "Love your neighbor as yourself." That commandment is at the heart of the Golden Rule.

I'll admit that it has not always been easy for me to feel love for the bullies who pick on me and say hurtful things, or for those who treat me as some sort of freak who is inferior or not worthy. I don't expect it will be easy for you to love and forgive your bullies either.

Then again, it doesn't have to be easy, and maybe, just maybe, God doesn't want it to be easy. He may want to test your strength and your faith by allowing a bully to get in your face or do something that hurts you. Knowing that may help you some, but maybe it's still not enough. I understand, and so does God. So think of the ultimate lesson in love and forgiveness. Think of Jesus on the cross looking up to heaven and saying, "Father, forgive them; for they know not what they do."

You may find that inspiring, but you may also argue that Jesus was the Son of God and you're just a teenager trying to survive. No one expects you to love a bully who is trying to do you serious bodily harm or to somehow humiliate or hurt you. Turning the other cheek may not be an option either. But later, when you are out of harm's reach, you can ask for God's help in making it possible to love and forgive your bully.

Don't do it for the bully's sake. Do it for your own. Ask God to grant you compassion for them. God has compassion for us even though He knows all our faults. He still chooses to love us. Maybe your bully lives in a troubled or abusive home without love and support.

I've often looked back and wondered if I could have made a radical difference by showing love for some of my bullies. That would have been interesting! It certainly would have been a radical move for a victim to show love to a bully, but that is exactly what Jesus did.

Your bullies may not know what to do if you show them compassion, offer them forgiveness, or reach out to them instead of running from them. I wouldn't advise doing this unless you have a good escape plan or lots of friends around. A fast motorcycle might be a good idea too. Keep the engine running!

> ## We were all created to be instruments of God's love.

Whether or not you express empathy for your bully, it might help you to think of your bully as someone's child who has somehow gone wrong. We were all created to be instruments of God's love, so I'm sure it is part of His plan that we let others know they are valued and appreciated.

I've wondered too if my bullies would have changed their

ways altogether if I had dared to offer them love instead of fear and dread. Maybe I could have saved someone else from being terrorized or driven to suicide.

The Fruit of Joy

It's hard to argue against joy. Who doesn't want to be joyful, right? But again, you may have a hard time feeling the joy when a bully is breathing down your neck, tossing rocks at you, cursing you, turning friends against you, excluding you from social events, or tormenting you with Facebook posts.

The key to this value is that you shouldn't expect other people to create joy for you. That's not to say that your closest friends, parents, siblings, and loved ones won't give you happiness and joy, but true and lasting joy comes from within you.

I derive great joy from my faith, from my work, from doing things for others, from having a positive impact on the world, and of course from my family and other loving relationships. You can tap the same sources of deep and lasting joy even if a bully is making your day-to-day life about as much fun as a fifty-page term paper.

When you generate joy from within, it can create a sort of bully-proof shield. Believe me, nothing gets a bully's goat more than someone who can smile and keep walking.

If someone brings joy to your life, that's a great gift, but know that you can create joy from within by savoring the blessings in your life whether it's the talents and gifts you've been given or the beauty of a sunset, a hug from your mom or dad, or the warm welcome of your puppy when you come home from school.

Bank all the joy you can find, and cash it in when bullies try to spoil your day. Those bullies may tear up your term paper, but they'll never steal your joy.

The Fruit of Peace

I'm sure anyone being dogged by a bully would give an arm and a leg for some peace. (No, that's not what happened to me.) But again, peace is a value that can be and should be generated from within if you can tap into your faith.

It's possible to feel peace within yourself even if someone is in your face threatening to mop up the floor with you. When I feel like the world is warring on me, I go to my place of peace built on my faith and trust in the goodness of God. There, I bask in His love, shutting out anger, frustration, and worries.

If you need peace because of a bully, know that the peace of God is yours to claim. In the Bible (John 14:27), Jesus explained that He was leaving us with this gift or legacy, which He described as the "peace of mind and heart." As Scripture says, true peace isn't something the world gives you. No one else can give you peace. It's a gift Jesus left us, one that rests within you and your heart.

So how do you tap into that faith? You ask God for it. Seek His plan for your life. Discover His forever reassuring love for you in Scripture. The Bible says that the hearing of the Word produces faith. That's why I do Bible study, because I always need to be refreshed in faith for the daily ups and downs.

When I went through a very difficult time in December 2010, I kept repeating Philippians 4:13 throughout the day: "I can do all things through Christ who strengthens me."

Whatever I can't do, I believe God can do in me and through me. That is truly the foundation of faith that has built me up and transformed me from the inside out.

The Fruit of Patience

I'm told someone once asked God for more patience and then had to wait in line for an hour while God thought about it. When he finally complained about the wait, God said, "You wanted patience, so I gave you the opportunity to practice it."

I've had many opportunities to practice patience, but I'm still trying to get it right. Patience is a virtue as well as a value. I have to confess I'm a little late in recognizing that. When I was a teen, and even as a single guy in my twenties, I was usually on my own schedule, doing what I wanted when I wanted to do it.

I definitely learned my first lessons in patience when I began living with caregivers. They were there to help me, but I had grown so used to helping myself that at first I had little patience with them. When I began traveling around the world, I always had a caregiver with me, so we were constantly together day and night. They had to be patient with me too, of course.

I'm sure it was harder for them than it was for me, but I was new to this experience, so I struggled a bit. Finally, I learned to be grateful for their presence and all the things they did for me, and that helped make me more patient. Patience is such a crucial virtue in life, and it has many layers and applications. It is hard to train your thoughts, control your emotions, and hold on to patience. Again, I still have a lot to learn, but I have definitely reaped the fruits of obtaining patience and asking God to give me more.

I didn't realize how much more I needed to learn about patience until Kanae and I married and started our family. When an older friend with kids heard we were having a child, he offered this urgent bit of advice: "Nick, hurry up and learn patience."

Teenagers have other challenges when it comes to practicing patience. Dealing with bullies requires using patience with perspective. When I was feeling beleaguered by high school bullies, my perspective was very short term. I thought their taunts and torments would never end. That limited perspective left me feeling overwhelmed and desperate. Whenever a bully bothered me, I had to escape immediately. I hid in the shrubbery so often I think some classmates thought I was a new species of plant.

> Dealing with bullies requires
> using patience with perspective.

Patience would have helped me greatly back then. With patience I would have had a clearer long-term perspective that would have relieved the stress. I was locked into thinking, *This bully is going to make me miserable for the rest of my life.* Patience would have told me, "This too shall pass."

The Bible's most famous example of patience is Job. Although Job was a wealthy man of great faith, for some reason God wanted to test his faith. So God allowed the devil to destroy all of Job's possessions and to take away his children too.

Job accepted that God had a plan in place and a reason for allowing so many bad things to happen to him. God allowed his faith to be tested to the point that even patient Job cried out to show that he was just as human as you and me. The lesson is that God rewarded Job's patience and faith by giving back to him twice what he'd had before.

The Fruit of Kindness

How can this fruit of the Spirit help you deal with bullies and the other challenges of your teenage years? It's a tough question for sure. When someone is taunting you, physically assaulting you, ostracizing you, or cyberbullying you, where does kindness come into play?

The Bible tells us in Luke 6:35 to "love your enemies, and do good, and lend, expecting nothing in return; and your reward will be great, and you will be sons of the Most High; for He Himself is kind to ungrateful and evil men." And Proverbs 16:7 says, "When a man's ways please the LORD, He makes even his enemies to be at peace with him."

I think the modern "street" translation of this might be "Kill 'em with kindness." Or maybe not! Seriously, I have tried being kind to my bullies, and sometimes it has worked while at other times it's only made them meaner.

Some bullies respond to kindness because deep down they are hurting and no one has ever shown them compassion. That's the case with so many young people I meet around the world. They are hurting. They have holes in their hearts because they live in violent households or their parents split up or they've been abandoned and put in one foster home after another.

Yet some people have the gift of kindness and compassion even if they have never experienced it themselves. In Mumbai and other impoverished places I've met sex slaves—teens kidnapped and forced into prostitution—who have amazed me with their kindness toward others, including me.

Maybe being kind to those who bully you won't make

them stop, at least right away. There are no guarantees. Some bullies are just cruel and angry people. But I think showing kindness is always worth a try, and actually, I think it's the best way to live in general. Even if you've never had anyone be kind to you, I suggest that you offer compassion to others and see what happens.

Great power can lie in just a few kind words. Sowing little acts of kindness can render huge harvests. A smile, a compassionate look, a phone call, or a hug can make someone's day and even save a life.

As a boy, I helped my father plant tomato seeds in our backyard. Then my father told me to watch the vines grow from those seeds. He said it would take a long time, so I watched it for three hours. I saw no change. The next day proved exactly the same.

I believed that if I watched it, the vine would somehow grow more quickly, but with every passing minute, it was my frustration that grew instead. I had no patience. I wanted instant results. My father should have given me a Chia Pet instead!

When I think of this childhood memory, I cannot help but relate it to the experience of kindness. We may get frustrated if it is not returned immediately, yet often a single kindness plants seeds that will one day grow and flourish into something far greater—maybe a friendship, maybe even love.

I believe that to offer kindness and love without expecting anything in return is a heroic act. It takes more courage to give without expectation than to give knowing that you will get something in return. One is an act of faith; the other is merely a transaction.

So be kind. Keep planting those seeds of love. If you don't have a friend, be a friend. Give a free hug. Give a free smile. You never know what will grow from your kindness. Sometimes magic happens. You may even turn a bully into a friend!

The Fruit of Generosity

We're told in the Bible that those who bless others with their generosity will themselves be blessed. To have a generous spirit is a great gift. Being generous to a bully might be difficult. It's hard to do nice things for someone who is making your life miserable. So I'm not saying you have to be generous to bullies. But if you are generous to others, you will feel better about yourself, and that makes it more difficult for bullies or anyone else to get to you.

Generosity moves you to help others. It also fits my philosophy that when you are in need, the best thing to do is serve the needs of others. The Bible supports this when it says in Proverbs 19:17, "Whoever is generous to the poor lends to the LORD, and he will repay him for his deed."

Teens may be tempted to say they don't have anything to

give, so generosity is not a value they can embrace. Sorry, but that is not true. The Bible tells us in Romans 12:6: "We have different gifts, according to the grace given us."

You may not have money or valuable possessions, but you are blessed with talents and time, which can be great blessings to others. Volunteering as a tutor, mentoring as a Big Brother or Big Sister, or assisting the elderly are all acts of generosity that require little more than giving your time and energy.

You should never give for your own gain, but that doesn't mean rewards won't come to you. God designed us so that when we are generous to others, our spirits are lifted.

When I was in my late teens and dealing with issues of self-doubt, questioning my value and my place in the world, I had this compelling desire to travel to South Africa and help the needy there. A young South African who'd heard me speak wanted to set up a tour of schools, orphanages, and prisons across the region.

My parents were naturally concerned for my safety and even more concerned for my sanity when I announced plans to take twenty thousand dollars that I'd saved for a house and give it away to the needy on the tour. Despite their concerns, I went to Africa and dispensed the funds, buying diapers, washers, dryers, and medical supplies for several orphanages we visited. I was saddened to see so many children without families but heartened by the strength of their spirits, their laughter, and their joy.

I thought I could make a difference in their lives, but—as so often happens when you practice generosity—instead they made a huge difference in mine. Really, that trip changed my life. My experiences there gave me the confidence and motivation to take on speaking engagements and missions around the world.

The contact in South Africa and the funds I'd made from speaking engagements put me in a unique position for that trip. I certainly wouldn't expect you to take on something of that magnitude. But you could practice generosity in your own school or community, doing service projects or working for a local Habitat for Humanity project or serving on a mission for your church.

> **Give your friendship to someone who feels alone and friendless.**

Another small act of generosity would be to offer up prayers for those in need. You and I can't perform miracles, but prayers connect us to Someone who can. Miracles may not be within our reach, but God's arms are longer than ours, especially mine!

One last act of generosity that I'll recommend to you is to give your friendship to someone who feels alone and friendless. When I travel and talk to teens around the world, one thing that strikes me is that more and more of them seem to feel isolated. They often communicate only over the Internet, through e-mails, texts, and tweets. The lack of true companionship is not a good thing.

There was a time in my life when I was very worried that no one would ever want to be my friend because I looked so much different than everyone else. One day, I had this thought: *If I only had just one really good friend, my life would be so much better.*

You can be that friend for someone else in need. You may even save that person's life, and who knows what rewards will come your way for your generosity.

The Fruit of Faithfulness

I posted a message on my Facebook page in May 2012 that said, "It is far better to be faithful with what you have than being distracted with the 'if only,' 'could've,' 'should've,' or 'would've' thoughts. Be thankful, learn, grow, and be faithful."

My thought on faithfulness must have struck a chord, because more than 3,000 people "liked" it and more than 570 shared it with their friends. Why is faithfulness so important to so many people, and why should it be important to you in dealing with bullies? This is another of those values that can't be directly applied as a defense against those who would mistreat you, but if you embrace it and take it to heart, faithfulness will make it much more difficult for bullies to rock your boat.

Faithfulness has several different meanings. To Christians, it is about living according to God's teachings and trusting in His unwavering goodness, love, and mercy, no matter what happens to us. Faithfulness is also a virtue or character trait. When you have it, faithfulness proves to those around you that you are filled with God's Spirit.

Do people think of you as a faithful person? a faithful friend? a faithful student, classmate, teammate, or employee? If not, it's because you aren't being who you claim to be. Somewhere along the line you've broken the bonds of trust that faithfulness strengthens.

Early in my life especially, I had to depend on the faithfulness of those who took care of me. My parents proved their faithfulness in caring for me and giving me the guidance I needed, even when I resisted it. Now my caregivers who help me deal with my disabilities display their faithfulness by showing up every day, doing their jobs, and standing by me even when I'm cranky and not much fun to hang out with. When my faithfulness needs a tune-up and I need to look at my priorities, I ask God to help me and I thank Him for being faithful to me.

To the world in general, faithfulness also means being loyal, reliable, trustworthy, and steadfast. Teens, and adults too, show faithfulness by doing what they say they will do, keeping promises, and being authentic by "walking the talk."

Don't let hurts or hard times throw you off track. Keep the faith. Know that you have value, and know that hurts fade and hard times give way to better days. I sort of panicked in my early teens, and as a result, I lost faithfulness in several areas of my life, wandering from some of my most important values and beliefs.

> Hurts fade and hard times
> give way to better days.

If you've made the same mistake, don't beat yourself up. Nobody is perfect. Be grateful that you still have the opportunity to get back on track, and then take steps to return to a more authentic and fulfilling lifestyle. Determine who could have been hurt by your actions or words, ask them for forgiveness, and also ask God for forgiveness and to renew your mind day by day.

The Fruit of Gentleness

The Bible has many references to gentleness as a desirable value. Galatians 6:1 even seems to offer advice on how to use gentleness when dealing with bullies. It says, "Brothers, if anyone is caught in any transgression, you who are spiritual should restore him in a spirit of gentleness. Keep watch on yourself, lest you too be tempted."

A modern interpretation of that might be: "Dude, if a bully

gets in your face, you should tell him to chill; just make sure you don't become a bully too."

I've never tried to use gentleness on a bully, but there is another scripture that says, "Let your gentleness be evident to all." Maybe that approach would work, but then again, maybe not. So what place does gentleness have in our efforts to bully proof you? Well, being a gentle spirit may not scare away your tormentors, but it might help you build a protective shield of friends and supporters whom bullies won't want to mess with.

Being gentle isn't about being weak. Jesus is often described as gentle and He certainly wasn't weak. He even threw the money-changers out of the temple. That was awesome! Being gentle is more about practicing humility, giving up the need to be right, putting other people first, being a good listener and a good friend, protecting those who are being abused, and comforting those in need.

I know you've heard phrases used like "gentle as a lamb" or "gentle as a dove" or even in commercials for laundry detergents that companies claim are "gentle as a mother's touch." But real gentleness, the value that we should all strive for, is much deeper than those phrases would indicate.

Many of the strongest and most admirable people I know are gentle spirits who don't have to prove how tough they are on the outside because they are so strong on the inside. People with that quality are my heroes. They have this calmness and quiet-ness about them, but you know their character and their faith are so strong that nothing rattles them.

When I was a teen, I had a tendency—okay, a really bad habit—of wanting to win every argument and especially to al-ways be right. If someone pointed out that I had a fact wrong, I'd still try to bull my way through it just so I could claim I was really right. One day a friend who was fed up with this bad habit of mine said, "Nick, just because you are right doesn't mean you have to tell me about it every time."

Zing! She killed me with kindness! She was both telling me and showing me that the real power lies in being gentle and kind and a good friend—not in being argumentative and forever in-sistent on being the authority on all things. Selfishness and pride can make us want to be heard and respected, but instead we lose touch with the value of gentleness and quiet strength.

The next time a bully darkens your path, don't take the bait and respond to taunts with your own harsh words. Instead, consider that maybe God is using the bully to test your inner strength, your quiet power—your ability to be every bit as gen-tle and strong as Jesus Himself.

The Fruit of Self-Control

A friend asked me to do some counseling with a young guy who had married into his family. Tim was barely into his twenties. He and his wife had been married a couple of years. They had two kids right off the bat, and Tim wasn't handling his new responsibilities very well. He hadn't made the switch from the mentality of a single guy who could do anything he wanted, anytime he wanted, to a married guy whose wife and children needed him to be there for them.

Tim also had admitted that he'd been in trouble at work, which had set off alarms in his wife's family. Basically, he lacked maturity and self-control. I told Tim he needed to be a better example for his kids. "You want them to be proud of you and to see you as a role model, don't you?" I asked. "As a father, you have to put their needs and their welfare above your own. It all comes down to self-control and realizing that your responsibilities have expanded."

We had a very friendly, deep discussion. He knew I was just trying to wake him up. I could see that Tim took it to heart, and his actions from then on reflected it. He has been a much better husband and father. He still has ups and downs when he needs to practice more self-control, but then most of us feel that we could benefit from more of this fruit of the Spirit.

The Bible says, "A man without self-control is like a city broken into and left without walls." As a teen, I can remember teachers constantly telling me and my classmates, "Okay, everyone, get it under control." It was strange to hear that back then, because like most teens, I didn't think I had control over much.

I lived with my parents. I had no job and no money. What did I control? Our dog didn't even listen to me most of the time!

Bullies don't have control over themselves. They taunt their targets, push them around, and socially isolate them because they are too weak to control their worst impulses and emotions in more productive ways. That's why using self-control in response to bullies can be so effective.

When you refuse to respond to taunts or you don't let a bully's shove trigger your own violence, it shows that you are operating at a higher level of maturity and self-control. If the bully continues to pursue you and you feel seriously threatened, you may have to defend yourself or flee or get help. I would never tell you to let a bully beat you up, but violence should be your last response. I'll offer more advice on this later in the book; for now I want to encourage you to adopt all the fruit of the Spirit as values and make them part of your daily approach to life.

We are born into this world kicking and screaming and demanding that our hunger and thirst and comfort be tended to. It would be nice if we could stay in that mode for the rest of our lives, but unfortunately, even the most doting parents get over the whole diaper-changing thing pretty quickly.

We may still have the same primitive urge to be the center of the universe, but as we enter the teen years, we're expected to keep many of our desires and cravings in check for our benefit and the benefit of everyone else. A lack of self-control leads to poor choices.

You can use self-control and still have fun; it's just a matter of doing things in moderation and knowing when to say enough. If you find yourself losing control or lacking it altogether when faced with a bully or an offer of drugs or the temptation of sex, you can ask God to provide you with the strength to stand strong and stay in control.

If you build your life on the bedrock values and virtues of love, joy, peace, patience, kindness, generosity, faithfulness, gentleness, and self-control, I have no doubt that you will reap the fruit of the Spirit. And I believe among the blessings you receive will be the self-confidence, courage, and resilience to deal with any bullying, ill treatment, or challenging circumstance that happens in your life.

Nick's Notes for Chapter Four

- Strong values can give you the strength to deal with bullying and other challenges throughout your life.
- We can all benefit by building our lives around values such as love, joy, peace, patience, kindness, generosity, faithfulness, gentleness, and self-control.

Five

Create Your Safety Zone

Establish inner security
and strength that make
you bully proof.

Once you accept that you have value and purpose, take responsibility for your own happiness, and build your life on strong values, you can create a safety zone where no bully, or any other person or event, can make you feel badly about yourself. Think of it as a safe room or a storm shelter that isn't in your house or your school. Instead, it exists within your mind. You can go there to feel secure in who you are whenever you encounter a threat from a bully or a bad experience of any kind.

This isn't about protecting yourself physically from bullies who want to hurt you by beating you up or otherwise harming you. I'll offer some advice on that later in the book. This safety zone is created to protect you emotionally so that you won't become stressed out or depressed by bullying or other negatives in your life.

Your safety zone may exist only in your consciousness, but its impact on your life can be very powerful. And it will always be there, no matter where you are, for the rest of your life. I taught myself to go to my own safety zone mentally when a bully or a bad experience shook my confidence or made me question my value and my future.

I'd go off by myself somewhere, mentally step into this shelter, and say to myself, "I am a child of God, and He created me for a purpose. He has a plan for my life. No one can take that away from me or make me feel diminished. I am loved, and I have value."

You may be thinking, *Well, that works for you, Nick, but it probably won't work for me.* So let me introduce you to Jenny, who happened to write an e-mail to my website describing what is essentially her own safety zone process. She doesn't call it that, but as you will see, it works much the same.

Jenny was teased and bullied in grade school and high school because, like me, she doesn't look like most other people. It's sad but true that she was not noticed for the beauty that was in her heart and mind; instead she was picked on and treated harshly because she was born with Apert syndrome.

After reading Jenny's e-mail, I had to look up Apert syndrome because I was not familiar with it. This seems like a cruel disability. Some studies say one in sixty-five thousand children born have it. Most have malformations of their skulls, faces, hands, and feet. I mentioned earlier that as a child I often felt sorry for myself because my disabilities were so obvious and couldn't be hidden. It's very humbling to think that Jenny dealt with a much more severe physical disability with such grace, though she admitted that she, too, had her bad days, as you might expect.

"Suffice it to say that it took much faith in God, the support of my family, especially my mom and dad and my sisters to help me figure out that I was OK despite what the 'world' thought," she wrote to me. "I LOVE YOUR testimony on this. I especially LOVE what you said on the *20/20* [television show] interview that 'it's not what the world thinks of you, but what YOU think of you.' I have lived by that same motto for a LONG time."

Jenny said she graduated high school, college, and grad school with good grades while also playing the trumpet and singing in her church choir. She also wrote that music plays an important role in her own safety zone, just as it does in mine. I often play music when I'm stressed out or feeling sad. I've done this since my teen years when I was bullied. Music soothes me, and Jenny said that it does the same for her.

"I don't know that I would be the same person had it not been for music," she wrote. "It's where I find my peace, my soul."

One of the great things about creating your own safety zone—whether in your mind or a special room or space—is that you can fill it with whatever puts your soul at peace: your favorite music, images of loved ones, prayers, inspirational messages, quotes from Scripture, or even mental or real images of your favorite inspirational people (I am available of course!). It's your "room," so feel free to decorate it any way you want.

> One of the great things about creating your own safety zone is that you can fill it with whatever puts your soul at peace.

Another valuable item that I recommend you take into your safety zone is your purpose or mission in life. If you haven't decided what that is yet, that's okay. Instead, bring along thoughts of your passion, whatever it is that you enjoy doing most. Let that feeling of happiness and fulfillment wash over you.

Think about how you might build your entire life around that passion. If it's music, maybe you could be an entertainer or a music teacher or work in the music industry. If you are a computer wizard, you have even more opportunities out there creating software or apps, developing new search engines or operating systems. Let your imagination take you away from what's troubling you now and into a much better future.

When you decide what your passions are—yes, you can have more than one—it becomes easier to find other people who share the same interests. Often you find them by joining clubs, teams, or hobby groups built around those shared passions. This is good for you on many levels, and it also builds up your bully defense system and gives you another room in your safety zone. You see, psychologists say the more social interactions we have—the closer we are to family members, and the more friends and acquaintances we have—the less likely it is that a bully can isolate us as targets.

It's also true that when you have a passion for something, it's usually because you are good at it or some aspect of it. That helps build your confidence and self-esteem, which are powerful additions to your bully defense system and your safety zone.

GETTING IN YOUR ZONE

I didn't realize until my high school years that I really enjoyed public speaking. When I was younger, I was terrified of going in front of my classmates and reading a paper or giving a speech. At that point, I was still very nervous and self-conscious about being different—and I'm not referring to my Australian accent. As I entered my teen years, my parents encouraged me to put myself out there a little bit so people would get to know me. I began speaking up in class and sharing my feelings with classmates.

To my surprise, the other kids didn't run when I spoke to

them. Many of them actually seemed to enjoy talking to me and learning more about me. Some of them wanted to be friends and hang out with me. A few even shared their feelings with me and confided in me about their own insecurities and fears.

When you grow up as different as Jenny and me, you tend to have a greater empathy for others. My disabilities made me more understanding and more sympathetic. I'm always willing to listen and offer encouragement and support. Those are qualities I never realized I had until my parents encouraged me to come out of my shell and to speak up more so my classmates could get to know me.

After a while, I actually found myself enjoying classes in which I had to give speeches or read my papers aloud. Slowly, I realized that I had a gift for communicating with people. Every time I dared to speak up or to sit down and let others share their feelings with me, I had this sense of being more engaged and alive. I don't know how else to describe it other than *thrilling*. Not in the sense that a scary ride at an amusement park is thrilling, but there are some similarities. It was an addictive sort of thrill. One I wanted to re-create time and time again. So I kept putting myself out there.

Then one day, a janitor at my high school told me I should think about becoming a professional speaker. That seemed like a crazy idea at first.

"What would I talk about?" I asked him. "Who would come to hear me?"

"Talk about the same thing you talk about to the kids in school," he said. "They love it when you share your stories with them about dealing with your disability, trying to fit in, and using your sense of humor to handle challenges."

This janitor didn't just clean up around the school. He was a very caring Christian guy who I became friends with and talked to most afternoons after school while waiting for my ride home. He suggested I come to a meeting as a guest speaker. I put him off for a while, but he finally convinced me to speak to a small group. They were very supportive and attentive. After that, I spoke to any group that requested my time. I probably spoke to a few who didn't even ask me. (Okay, so I sometimes stood on street corners just talking to myself.)

Before I knew it, I was speaking to a group of three hundred people and I was being invited to speak to organizations and schools in other communities.

You know the rest of the story. The point is that I discovered a passion and I've built my life around that passion. More importantly, I found my purpose—to encourage and inspire others—and that is one of the most powerful things I take into my safety zone.

From my earliest days as a speaker just talking to classmates,

I discovered that one of the things that kept me from becoming sad or discouraged when someone picked on me or something bad happened was just thinking about my last speech or the next one coming up. People told me they enjoyed my talks. They said my story inspired them. They thanked me, but in truth, they gave me much more than I'd given them. They confirmed my value on this earth. I took that to the bank—and into my safety zone.

THE REALM OF POSSIBILITY

When I first read Jenny's e-mail, I realized that she had followed a similar path and that her own career was something she kept as a source of comfort in her safety zone.

"I am a social worker and counselor for a major medical health system in…Georgia," she wrote. "I work for an outpatient case management department—managing cases for the poorest of the poor in one of the rural counties…. It is my JOY—I LOVE my job."

Jenny's next sentence is the one that convinced me that she, too, has a safety zone where she goes to protect herself and to tap into all the good things in her life instead of focusing on the bad. She calls it "the realm." Here is how she described it: "I believe that you can live in the realm that God may one day heal you or me, but…if God doesn't, this is what God meant for me and that's OK. That's absolutely OK! More importantly, I am here with Apert's for GOD's own reason—GOD meant this and that's really what matters."

"The realm that God may one day heal you or me." That's Jenny's safety zone. God can use all things to work together for the good of those who love Him and have been called according to His purpose. Take comfort in knowing that He is with us and can bring a greater purpose in the difficult times.

Jenny goes to her safety zone with her music and the good feelings from her fulfilling work, and she shuts out the negatives in her life while focusing on the positives and the future. You can call your safety zone whatever you want. Just make good use of it because it is a very valuable thing to have—and a great place to go when bad people or hard times are stressing you out.

> You are one of God's children,
> fearfully and wonderfully made.

Let's look at ways to help you create your own safety zone, and let's think about what you can take with you when you mentally enter that zone to seek comfort, encouragement, security, and value. Write your answers on a separate sheet of paper. Keep it around so when a bully picks on you or hard times hit, you'll have a reminder to help furnish your special place for boosting your spirits, hope, faith, and self-worth.

One of the Bible passages I take into my safety zone is Psalm 139:13–14, which says, "For you created my inmost being; you knit me together in my mother's womb. I praise you because I am fearfully and wonderfully made; your works are wonderful, I know that full well."

I also carry into my safety zone thoughts of my ministry through Life Without Limbs. God has used me in countless schools, churches, prisons, orphanages, hospitals, stadiums,

Creating Your Safety Zone

1. What do people say they like about you?
2. What do your parents, friends, or teachers most often compliment you on?
3. What do you enjoy doing more than anything else?
4. What soothes your spirit and engages you mentally and physically so that you lose track of everything else?
5. How can you build your life around those things that fulfill you and help you feel like you are making a contribution or a difference?
6. What is the best possible future you can envision for yourself?
7. Who loves you unconditionally?

and in face-to-face encounters with individuals, telling them how very precious they are to Him. You are one of God's children, fearfully and wonderfully made. No one can take that away from you. God has a plan for each and every life. Our lives are meaningful and purposeful because His hand guides everything we do when we have faith. God took my life, one that others might disregard as not having any significance, and filled me with His purpose and showed me His plans. Through Him, I have moved hearts and lives toward Him.

8. What scriptures, music, movies, books, works of art, photographs, pets, or activities make you forget your troubles and worries and give you peace?

9. What do you love to do so much that you want to do it for the rest of your life? How can you make a living doing it?

10. What is the nicest thing anyone has ever done for you? How can you do something similar for another person?

11. What friend or family member needs encouragement right now? How can you reach out to that person?

12. What would it feel like to be part of the safety zone for another person?

13. How can your faith in God help you right now? What prayers work best for you when you are feeling stressed or scared?

God has a plan for your life too. And that is your ultimate safety zone!

Nick's Notes for Chapter Five

- You can create a safety zone within your mind where you can go mentally and emotionally to soothe yourself and build strength when bullies come around or other challenges arise.

- Short-term thinking can make being bullied seem even worse, so when you go into your safety zone, find peace by looking ahead to better days and a future of unlimited opportunities. Things may seem bad right now, but this too shall pass.

Six

Build Your Backup

Build strong and supportive relationships for backup against bullying.

When I was in my early teens, I thought of my bullies as enemies, people who wanted to hurt me with their words or actions. I never considered that a bully could be someone I thought of as a friend until I starting hanging out with Zeke. This was in high school when I was trying to fit in by acting tough, cursing all the time, and ignoring the other Christian kids in my school. For some reason, the opinions and friendship of the non-Christian, pot-smoking, foulmouthed kids were important to me. They weren't terrible people. Some of them had very good hearts. Many of them had tough home lives and were trying to deal with problems they weren't equipped to handle. So I'm not putting them down.

I wish I could have helped them, but at that point, I needed help myself. I had lost my way, lost touch with my faith, and I was pretending to be some other guy who was really nothing like the real me.

Some bullies are subtler than others. They don't get in your face and threaten you. Instead, they do their best to manipulate you to serve their own interests. Street gangs often work in this way. They identify someone who is isolated, from a broken family with little parental supervision, and they move to fill the emotional need to be supported and protected. Then, once they have recruited the needy or lost person, they manipulate their new member into doing their dirty work, which may include selling drugs, carrying weapons, beating people, robbery, and other crimes.

These bully "friends" also may try to tell you who you are and what you should do. I let that happen to me for a while. I let others influence how I acted and what I thought of myself. I listened to them instead of that voice inside telling me, *This is wrong. You're not like this.*

I finally realized I'd wandered far from the real me when Zeke, an older classmate, offered me a cigarette. I may have started swearing to fit in, but I drew the line at ruining my health. It's hard enough having no limbs, but there's no way I could survive without good lungs.

It struck me as odd that anyone would look at me or know me even a little and think I'd smoke a cigarette. It's fairly obvi-ous, or should be, that I'm not exactly built to be a smoker—unless they've come up with some sort of hands-free cigarette that I haven't heard about!

When Zeke first suggested that I smoke, I thought, *He*

doesn't have a clue as to who I am. A little later, it hit me that I really didn't know who I was either; otherwise, I wouldn't have wanted him as a friend.

Again, I'm not putting Zeke down. He wasn't a bad person. He just wasn't the sort of person I needed to be hanging out with.

> **People respond to you and treat you according to the way you act, not the way you think or feel.**

It wasn't his fault. He assumed I'd like to smoke cigarettes because I'd been presenting myself as that kind of guy—the guy who cursed and acted tough. This was the first time I realized one of the key facts about relationships: people respond to you and treat you according to the way you act, not the way you think or feel.

I may have thought I was still a straight-arrow Christian, but that wasn't the way I'd been acting. That was clear when he pulled out the cigarette, offered it to me, and said, "Nick, your life must be sh**. I'd be really p***** off if I were you, and I'd want to smoke to help me chill out."

I couldn't figure out how smoking a cigarette would dramatically improve my life or reduce any anger issues I might have had. Maybe it's just me, but it doesn't sound relaxing to stuff a burning, paper-wrapped leaf in my mouth so smoke will fill my lungs. I knew people who smoked. Whenever they'd light up around me, the smoke made me cough. It made my clothes stink. I couldn't understand how any of those things would help me chill out.

My parents had taught me that smoking was bad for my health and that it could destroy my body, which is the temple of God. With all of that in mind, it wasn't tempting for me at all.

"No thanks. I'm fine," I told Zeke.

"Are you sure?" he said. "I'll hold it for you."

Zeke thought he was doing me a favor. His offer was actually touching, if misguided. This tough guy was reaching out, trying to show that he sympathized and wanted to help.

"No, I'm cool," I said.

He never asked me again. I reckon Zeke would not have asked me in the first place if I hadn't given him the impression that smoking might appeal to me. I was putting on a false front and running with a crowd of people who did not bring out the best in me. Some of them, whether intentionally or not, tried to lead me down the path of smoking cigarettes and pot.

Drinking alcohol and taking more serious drugs likely would have been next if I hadn't come to my senses and returned to a circle of friends whose values were much more in line with who I really was—or should have been.

It's true that I didn't have any outside bullies trying to

intimidate me or lead me astray while I was running with the tougher crowd for that short period in high school. Then again, some of my so-called friends from that crowd were subtly nudging me down a path that would have made me more vulnerable to bullying and manipulation.

Friends for Better or Worse

Most people consider themselves lucky if they have one or two friends they can count on. So don't put pressure on others or on yourself to create this huge circle of close friends. That's a rare thing to have in a world where people move around so much. If you have a bunch of buds, that's wonderful, but even one true friend is a great blessing. The most important thing is to be a friend to yourself, and part of that is to be careful who you hang with.

Your friends can be the best influences in your life. Or they can be the worst. They can protect you from bullying, or they can bully you themselves. That is why it is so important to choose your friends carefully.

Here is my simple guideline to choosing my closest friends and associates: the people I want to keep close and trust the most are those who make me want to be better, smarter, more loving, more open minded, more collaborative, more trustworthy, more empathetic, more faith filled, more God loving, more grateful, more forgiving, and more open to opportunities to serve God and those around me.

> A bully can steal only what you put out there for the taking.

These are the type of friends who will make you and me bully proof. Bullies are less inclined to pick on someone who has a big circle of friends, but even if a bully jumps out of the bushes and ruins your day, it won't matter over the long run because your close friends will have your back.

A bully can steal only what you put out there for the taking. If you have friends who make you feel good about yourself, who support you and encourage you and challenge you to be the best you can be, then no bully can take that away from you.

Your backup team includes friends who are close to your age and also other key people such as your parents, relatives, teachers, coaches, and clergy leaders. All of them should be positive, trustworthy, supportive, and inspiring. They should make you want to be your best and do your best.

HAVE YOU GOT BACKUP?

Have you ever taken the time to assess whether the friends and other people close to you are good or bad for you? I'd suggest you do that. On a separate sheet of paper make a list of the most important people in your life, the biggest influences, and those you spend the most time with. Then for each of them ask these questions:

1. Do we have mutual respect? Why or why not?
2. Do we trust each other? Why or why not?
3. Does this person encourage and support me?
4. Does our relationship make me want to be a better person?
5. If a bully confronted me, would this person stand by me?
6. What can I learn from this person?
7. Do I need to be a better friend to this person, or should I back off?
8. Is this someone I will be close to for a long time?
9. Do we share the same basic values?
10. Do we have equal power in the relationship, or is one of us more dependent than the other?
11. Does this person ever encourage me to do negative things that I would never do otherwise?
12. Am I comfortable talking about my faith with this person?
13. Is this someone who will celebrate my successes or be jealous of them?

When you have answered these questions for each of the

people closest to you, look over your responses. Consider whether you need to get closer to the positive influences and farther from those who aren't so positive. It's important to be aware of the nature of each relationship you have because sometimes we fall into comfort zones and hold on to relationships that don't serve us well and may even be harmful.

ARE THE FEELINGS
AND THE FRIENDSHIP MUTUAL?

Please remember also that you can't ask others to do for you what you wouldn't do for them. In fact, I would advise you to give more than you receive to those who support and encourage you. Think of your friendship as a refrigerator you share with a roommate. If you take out bread and sandwich meat for lunch, you need to add some later to be a good roomie. I can't stress enough how important it is to have positive people in your life and just how dangerous it is to hang out with those who don't bring out the best in you and maybe even drag you down below your worst.

A teen named Lester wrote to me about his own experiences with this. He described himself as "a rebel child that lived in a broken home.... Over the years, that killed me inside for always being scared and I was never happy. I was bullied when

I was small because I was chubby, and over the years I always had a really low self-esteem."

Instead of finding friends who helped him feel better and want better for himself, Lester started hanging out with a group of people who brought him down even more.

"I drank alcohol because I thought nobody loved me.... I was looking for happiness in the wrong places. I thought sex, getting girls, alcohol, going to parties, illegal street racing, and pornography was my way out to be happy."

Lester was headed for serious trouble. His friends were leading him toward a crash and burn. Fortunately, he took a detour that may have saved his life and his afterlife. He found a new circle of friends, including the most important friend of all. He attended a Christian youth convention "where I learned and felt through the Holy Spirit that Jesus Christ loves me and has never left my side.... It totally changed my life.

"God told me there that I was chosen because I heard His voice to serve Him...100%. I'm studying the Bible right now and reading daily to improve my messages I speak to the youth. Me and my brother are filming a documentary [about] how teenage lives...are today. I also have a youth group that 15 people attend. I live in an area where there are a lot of broken families. Many teenagers are lost and right now my whole life is dedicated to help. I know my purpose...is to be an example to the youth."

Purpose Brings Backup

As Lester discovered, there is true power in having a purpose. It's like this magnetic force that attracts others with similar passions. Ever since I declared my purpose in life by creating Life Without Limbs and traveling the world to inspire hope and ignite faith, I have been constantly amazed at the way people from around the world come into my life to support and join me in my mission.

One of them, Ignatius Ho, is a successful accountant and businessman in Hong Kong who is extremely passionate about everything he does, especially in matters of faith. He also has strong feelings about encouraging young people to find their purpose. He has two teenage sons, including one with autism, so Ignatius is especially attuned to those with disabilities.

When he saw one of my videos on YouTube about six years ago, Ignatius decided God wanted him to help me share my message in his native China. I didn't know this man at all, but his sincerity, selflessness, and high energy won my trust. He is a force of nature.

I joke that if you look up *faith in action* in the dictionary, you will see a picture of Ignatius because he is all about making things happen. When this human dynamo decided he wanted me to tour China, there was no stopping him. He took out a mortgage on his home, sold his car, and rallied support from a few churches in order to rent the stadium for my first event. Many people told him he was crazy because few Chinese would come to hear a foreigner speak about his Christian faith.

Ignatius told me, "I was forced to give up all my rational thinking and rely totally on God. I had no plan B. There was only a plan A and God would make the way." His hard work and sacrifices paid off. That event proved to be one of the most amazing days of my life! The stadium was filled beyond capacity. Thousands of people gave their lives to Christ.

Today, Ignatius leads our Hong Kong office and oversees our ministry to all of China and most of Asia. When he first contacted me and we met in 2008, Ignatius expressed his belief that young people in Asia needed to hear my message of faith, hope, and determination. Now, he helps me do that in a big way.

"In our culture, people always compare with each other and they can easily focus on what they don't have, their limitations," Ignatius said.

He believes that their culture leads Asian parents to focus on improving the faults of their children while they tend to neglect encouragement and praise for their children's achievements and strengths. Asian parents also tend to tell their children what careers to choose, focusing on income instead of allowing the kids to find their own paths based on their own dreams and passions, Ignatius says.

"Money comes first, and most parents suppress the free will of kids in telling them what to study and what career path to choose," he said. "That is why our young generation is not happy and feels lost when it comes to a purpose in their lives."

Ignatius, who has dedicated much of his life to encouraging young people to have hope and to follow their dreams, quickly became my biggest advocate and supporter in Asia. He has organized several tours for me that have covered more than a dozen countries in his part of the world. As you can imagine, these tours are very complex operations, yet I've learned there is no challenge Ignatius can't overcome through sheer force of will.

Your backup team members also want to see you grow and exceed your own expectations. Along with arranging my Asian tours, Ignatius, a lover and supporter of music, has encouraged me to pursue my interest in music, helping me release an album of children's songs.

My humble friend is the founder of two music charities in Hong Kong. His Music Angel Program brings renowned musicians and their music to children with disabilities throughout Asia. Ignatius also founded the Metropolitan Youth Orchestra of Hong Kong, which provides instruction and performance opportunities for more than 250 young musicians from 120 schools. The MYO musicians, whose motto is Music Excellence with a Soul, perform around the world, often for charity events in collaboration with renowned conductors and the finest musicians.

When you build your backup team, keep in mind that it can have a snowball effect. One good friend tends to attract others. That's exactly what happened when I joined forces with Ignatius. Working with him in Asia led me to another wonderful and supportive friend, Mr. Vu, a wealthy businessman in the steel industry who has become my biggest supporter in Vietnam.

Mr. Vu shares our passion for encouraging young people to overcome obstacles. One thing you may find with your backup, which is true of my relationship with Mr. Vu, is that you don't have to share everything as long as you share one major passion.

> One good friend
> tends to attract others.

Mr. Vu is not a Christian. He is a devout Buddhist. Yet he doesn't focus on how we differ in our faith. Like a true friend, he focuses on what we share. He has worked his tail off to set up tours of Vietnam for me, and the success of those trips has amazed us both. He put up more than one million dollars of his own money to lease a stadium for one event. We thought it would be a fairly small event with a couple thousand people, but more than thirty-five thousand showed up. Later, Mr. Vu flew us to Cambodia for more appearances.

FINDING BACKUP

These two men are now major members of my backup team in Asia and around the world. Both of them were drawn to my purpose to elevate lives and ignite hope. Your backup team will likely grow in the same way as you identify what it is you are passionate about and work to follow your purpose. In the meantime, if you are having trouble finding friends, as I mentioned earlier, look to groups, clubs, and organizations that are in line with your interests and passions.

One of the best things you can do for yourself and for your bully defense system is to be as strong and as healthy as you can be. This works on several levels. If you get strong and fit, you put yourself in a position to participate in athletics with teammates who can become friends and provide you with backup. Being strong physically is also great for your self-confidence. Bullies don't usually pick on those who look fit and exude confidence.

Taking self-defense classes is another way to get fit, make friends, and strengthen your bully defense system. You don't have to be a big person or incredibly strong to practice martial arts. The training is often designed to help smaller people protect themselves from larger attackers.

If you are physically capable, I recommend taking martial arts classes, especially those that focus on defending yourself without causing great harm to your opponent. I don't like physical violence, but I've had to protect myself as best I can on occasion, and the more you know about the art of self-defense, the more capable and confident you will be if a bully is intent on hurting you physically.

One of the best things about martial arts training is that it builds self-confidence and teaches you how to remain calm when threatened. Many bullies will back down when they see someone isn't easily threatened, especially if their intended victim uses training to easily break free of a wrist grab or headlock.

Look for a martial arts program that is designed to help you protect yourself rather than one that is all about combat, hurting people, or fighting competitively. Many martial arts instructors suggest jujitsu classes for teens faced with bullying because most forms of it teach methods for breaking free from attackers who try to grab you, put you in a headlock, choke you, pull you away, or bear hug you.

If I could take martial arts, I'd like to try something like aikido, which uses elements of jujitsu but focuses more on pure self-defense with methods that enable you to protect yourself without seriously hurting your attacker. Aikido is cool because you are taught to use the attacker's strength and momentum to repel the attack and prevent injury to yourself. You don't have to be superstrong or a big person to learn to use aikido, so it's especially good for those of us whom bullies like to pick on.

There are many benefits of self-defense martial arts. Training also stresses self-discipline, risk-assessment skills, coordination, flexibility, and strength, all of which are very beneficial.

Even if you don't hurt your bully, once the bully sees that you have martial arts skills, you probably won't have any more problems with that person trying to attack you. Another major benefit is that your self-defense classmates will become friends willing to stand by you and support you, which is a big deterrent to bullies. Remember, you should fight only if attacked and left no choice. I don't say that because I'm soft hearted. I've known people who got into fights over minor things only to have the other person pull out a knife or a gun and nearly kill them—or kill them. That's why I don't advocate jumping into a fight with your bully unless you have no other choice.

Reaching Out

It can be difficult to find and make friends if you're the new kid or if you have an obvious disability. I've been in both of those situations and sometimes more of them all at once. Imagine being the new kid in school who is also the only student without arms and legs, as well as the only one in a wheelchair and the only one with an Australian accent!

It didn't help that I did a really dumb thing when my parents moved us to the United States from Australia the first time. I worked very hard to cover up my Australian accent and sound American. Then a couple of months into the school year, I discovered that American girls loved Australian accents! You can believe I went all-out Aussie after that, mate.

> There is not a person in this world who hasn't felt different or alienated.

I made the mistake of trying to hide my accent, just as I once tried to hide my faith to fit in with the cool crowd at school. That sort of thing rarely works out well. You can't hide who you are. You can't deny what you truly believe. So my advice is to be yourself and make an active effort to find people who are willing to accept the real you. We all feel lonely at some points in our lives. There is not a person in this world who hasn't felt different or alienated at one time or another. The good news is you can do something about that, and you should. The first step is to stop waiting for the world to come to you and to reach out on your own.

Here is testimony from a teen who wrote to Life Without Limbs about coming out of his shell:

Being a paraplegic myself since the age of 3, I have battled with self-acceptance, acceptance from others and [heartbreak] for a situation I can't change. With God's given faith I have come out of my shell as I have now accepted positively who I am and [I am eager] to use my life experiences to serve God's purposes in my life. Looking back in my life I'm indeed blessed with supportive family who fought for...my rights, friends who look beyond my disabilities and became my closest friends.

This story hit home with me because I spent my teen years feeling much the same way as I tried to accept my circumstances and myself. My parents always pushed me to reach out to my classmates. They encouraged me: "You're a fun guy, Nick. People will like you, but you can't always expect them to come to you first. Sometimes you have to reach out to them. Speak up in class. Talk to the other kids. Help them get to know you!"

I hated to admit it, but my parents were right. (Sometimes they'd get lucky that way!) When I joked around in class and smiled and talked to kids in the hallway, they got over the fact that I was in a wheelchair and minus a few parts. They were much more accepting of me than I'd ever imagined they would be.

If you are ever in a situation where you are the new kid in school or in town or at work, do me a favor: don't pull a Nick and try to hide in the bushes. That doesn't help anything, and besides, there are mosquitoes there! Have you ever been eaten alive by mosquitoes? Now imagine being eaten alive by mosquitoes and not having any hands to scratch with! It's torture!

Instead of hiding and isolating yourself even more, make it your mission to make friends. Don't try too hard. Don't do what a kid in my school used to do and offer a quarter to anyone who'll be your friend. (I held out for fifty cents!) Instead, join organizations geared toward your interests so you can meet people who have those same interests. Volunteer your time for charitable groups, church groups, community events, or causes you believe in. It's all about finding common ground and building up from there. You don't have to impress people. Just be yourself and let them figure out how cool you are.

> Loneliness afflicts us all,
> but it's not terminal.

It takes courage and patience to put yourself out there. Believe me, I know. But the more friends you have, the less vulnerable you will be to life's bullies and hard times. Loneliness afflicts us all, but it's not terminal. You can kick it. Be open to the possibility that there are other human beings on this planet who might want to be friends with you. You may be more lovable than you think!

Anna, who lives in the British Isles, sent to our Life Without Limbs website her story of struggling to fit in. I found it very inspiring, and I hope you do too. Anna demonstrates a wonderful spirit in this story. She also shows great courage and determination. Rather than feeling sorry for herself and playing the victim, she reached out, made friends, and found the ultimate backup:

I have hypotonia (low muscle tone) which basically means that my muscles are weak and I am not able to do the same things as other people can do.... I got picked on because of this, and not just by other children but by the PE staff too; they never understood that I had a disability and continually put pressure on me to put more effort into what I was doing even though I was putting in all that I could. In my second [to] last year of high school I moved to a different school because I couldn't take any more and because I didn't have any friends there....

At this school there was a special unit for people to go into if they felt too uncomfortable to go outside with the others and for people who needed help with reading, writing etc. I had just been there for a week and I made so many friends, and people there appreciated me. It was wonderful and they were so understanding and I didn't have to worry about anything.

One day one of the friends that I made told me about this youth club at [a] church…and thought it would be good for me to go because it would help build my confidence etc. I was a bit nervous about going at first but I did and I haven't ever regretted it. I did sort of hide in a corner for the first few weeks that I went but as time went on I became more relaxed. As part of the youth club there is a ten-minute talk/discussion on Christianity. Now, I am from a non-Christian family so I didn't know that much about it but I never actually thought that there wasn't a God, I always thought that before I can make up my mind that I should learn more about it. So through spotlight (the youth cafe) and helping out doing arts and crafts at the holiday clubs.… I began to think maybe there is someone out there. So I went to one of the boys…at [the] holiday clubs and told him this and he gave me a small book on prayer and told me to take it home to look at and to tell him what I thought.

I took it home and that night I closed my bedroom door and began to pray for the very first time and it felt

wonderful as if God was with me. Since then I have
been praying, reading the Bible, going to Bible study
groups etc. Then one day I decided to get baptized to
show my love for God and our Lord Jesus Christ and
I have been a Christian ever since and do you know
what my dad came to my baptism, said at the start he
wouldn't stay for the whole thing but he did. He stayed
for the lunch, got to know/meet people who were there
and he enjoyed himself. He hasn't gone to any other
services but I just pray that over time he will and so
will the rest of my family, over time.

Looking back to what I have seen on some of the
videos by Nick I see and remember just how wonderful
God and the Lord Jesus is and that it doesn't matter
who we are or what we look like or what people may
think about us, that we are special, we are unique and
God loves us just the way we are.

Anna discovered something wonderful when she made the
choice not to feel sorry for herself and not to be lonely anymore.
She discovered that the first step to making friends is to be a
friend to yourself. Accept that you have value, that you are worthy of love and trust. Know that God loves you so that you will
never be alone or unloved, and then take that knowledge and
self-acceptance and make yourself available. Let other people

see the wonderful person God created you to be. It worked for Anna, and it will work for you too!

Nick's Notes for Chapter Six

■ Strong and supportive relationships are your greatest defenses against bullying and other challenges. Mutually supportive friendships are invaluable. The best friends are those who want the best for you, so that just knowing them and being around them will make you want to be your best too.

■ Teens often want to have a whole posse of friends to run around with. And if you have a big circle of friends you can trust, that's great, but having even one mutually supportive and trusting relationship is a great blessing.

■ The best way to attract and build friendships is to be a good friend to others.

Seven

Defeat the Bullies Inside

Monitor and manage your emotions to successfully deal with bullying.

o you remember the last time a bully gave you a hard time? Did the person say something mean, threaten you physically, start a rumor, post an unflattering picture online, or turn other people against you? Try to create a clear picture in your mind of exactly what happened.

Now think about how you felt. What emotions rose up? Did you feel hurt? anger? despair? depression? frustration? all of the above? anything else?

Okay, now think about what you did in response to the bully's actions or words. Did it make things better or worse? Did that bully stop bothering you? After you responded, did you feel better or worse? What would you have done differently?

Feel free to write down your responses to all my crazy questions on a sheet of paper. Many people find that writing things down helps them work out problems. It's also a good way to begin monitoring your negative emotions, so that instead of just responding emotionally, you can think first and respond more thoughtfully—which is always the best way to go.

In the Bible, Proverbs 16:32 tells us that it is "better to be slow to anger than to be a mighty warrior, and one who controls his temper is better than one who captures a city."

We have emotions for a reason. They don't just come over us by chance, even though it sometimes may seem that way. Asking where your emotions come from and assessing why you feel the way you feel are critical parts of creating self-awareness and asserting self-control over your actions.

It's important to know what triggers your emotions so you can better control your responses in ways that benefit you over the long term. Managing negative emotions is an important part of your bully defense system, and it is also a key to living a more successful life. People who let their negative emotions control their actions tend to feel out of control, insecure, and unhappy. Those who act based on a thoughtful process for monitoring and managing such emotions tend to be more successful, more confident, and happier.

Notice I didn't tell you that you should control your negative emotions. This is because you really can't control those feelings. The part of the brain that creates emotional responses has its own control room, and you don't have a key. Sorry, but that is not an excuse to shove an entire pie in your sister's face when she makes fun of you! You are still responsible for your actions.

People often are confused about the difference between controlling bad feelings and controlling actions. When we are very young, most of our emotional reactions are the result of triggers hard wired into our DNA, because over the centuries of human development, they were proven to help us survive in an often-hostile world.

As we get older, we have experiences upon which we form judgments so our emotional responses become more individualized. They are still automatic responses—meaning we have no control over them—but they are based on our value judgments and therefore may not be the correct responses. For example, you may fear someone based on a false story you heard about her. Or you may be naturally drawn to a man you don't know because he looks like your favorite uncle.

Emotions are useful in that they allow us to make very fast value judgments at times when fast responses are needed; for example, reacting quickly when you see an alligator swimming toward you with its jaws opened wide. But negative emotions can be bullies that push you to do crazy things that might hurt you and your relationships. You should first seek to understand what is behind the negative emotion before deciding how to respond to it. If you realize the feelings are based on incorrect information—the girl really isn't a bully or the man isn't your uncle—then you need to figure out how to respond accordingly.

When a mean dog appears out of nowhere and starts snarling and snapping its teeth in your direction, you feel scared. Your heart starts pounding. You breathe more rapidly. Maybe the hair on the back of your neck stands up or your face reddens.

All those physical responses are triggered by the same warning system that set off your feelings of fear. You can't control those feelings or the initial physical response, but if you see that the dog is on a leash, chained to a stake in the ground, or just a poodle with a big-dog bark, you can manage your response to the emotions accordingly.

Often you do this without thinking about it. You take a deep breath and get your breathing under control, slowing it down, which helps your heart rate slow down too. Maybe you laugh at yourself for being so frightened since we often use humor to release stress. You might even shout out, "Phew! That pit bull scared me."

Do you see what's happening here? When you realize the dog is not a serious and immediate threat, you recognize your emotions as invalid and adjust your response! It's a very natural process, and you can do the same thing when confronted by a bully—even if the bully does pose a threat. You have that power, and it's a good one to use.

Later in the book, I'll offer guidance on several ways to respond to bullies and which ways may be best for you in particular. For now, I want to give you the gift of emotional awareness and the power to choose your physical responses to your emotions.

THE SPACE BETWEEN FEELING AND ACTING

Emotions are natural and you feel what you feel. But the quality of your life is greatly affected by the choices you make in responding to your feelings. You see, a space, a time interval, and an opportunity lie between the point at which you feel something and the point at which you act on that feeling.

> The quality of your life is greatly affected by the choices you make in responding to your feelings.

This space is a gift. I'm not kidding about that. Psychologists say people who learn to use this space wisely are generally much more successful in life than those who either ignore it or don't use it well. This is the space where you can take control, make smart decisions, and put yourself in a position to determine your own destiny.

So when you get angry at a bully or your parents, you don't have to lash out. You can choose instead to step into that space between feelings and actions and ask some very helpful questions, such as:

- *Why am I angry?*
- *Is lashing out the best response? Will it help more or hurt more?*
- *What are my alternatives?*
- *What can I say to make things better?*
- *What can I say that will be beneficial for the long term?*

When you use the space to think about your response and to decide what is best for you over the long term, you are practicing self-awareness and self-control. This is called "response flexibility," and it is a sign of emotional intelligence.

This is really very simple to do, and after you do it several times, it can become a habit, a very good habit. The basic idea is just to think before you act on negative feelings or emotions so that you can figure out the best response for that particular situation. If a bully gets in your face, the best response is probably not to scream back or to get physical.

Easy for me to say, right?

Sure, the easy thing to do is to respond emotionally, but is it the smartest thing to do? Will it cause you only more grief and maybe even physical pain? Would the smarter response be to calmly talk to the bully to defuse the situation? Or would it be smarter to get a safe distance from the bully as quickly as possible?

Every situation is unique, so there is no one answer regarding the best response. But by mentally stepping into the space between your feelings and your action, you can better assess the situation, let go of the emotion, and more logically figure out your best options.

THE BULLY IN YOU

Here's something to consider: your negative emotions can be like bullies inside you. They try to provoke a response from you that may not be in your best interest. So if you simply do what those bad feelings stir you to do, you are just giving in to another bully in your life.

This thought occurred to me after I read an e-mail sent to my website by Dominic, who said he was fifteen years old and lived in Southeast Asia. When I read his story, I saw that at first Dominic let negative emotions bully him into doing things that weren't in his best interest. He gave in to that inner bully and it didn't work out very well for him, but later, when he thought about his response, he did something that helped him a lot.

When Dominic was in the ninth grade, he liked a girl and thought she liked him too. Then he found out she liked another guy who was a friend of Dominic's. That made him feel angry and depressed, so he shut both of them out of his life.

Dominic felt even worse after the girl and his friend became a couple. He would see them being affectionate at school and become even more depressed and angry. It didn't help that other classmates knew he'd liked the girl and they talked about how he'd lost her to his friend. That made Dominic feel like a failure, he said.

"I didn't have anyone. I cried from time to time, my grades went downhill and I dulled my pain with alcohol," he wrote. "I started to believe what people said about me, that I was a failure and not worthy to live, that I should just die, disappear, go away."

Dominic couldn't help feeling sad about his situation, but he let his feelings bully him into acting in a self-destructive way, didn't he? He said in his e-mail that he first realized there were more positive ways to respond after watching one of my videos on YouTube. He saw that I'd overcome my emotional inner bullies brought on by my disabilities and made the decision to lead a more positive life. Dominic began changing his response to his own feelings and changed his life in the process.

One day, after the school prom, he and the girl and her boyfriend patched things up by apologizing to each other. They forgave each other and closed the door on what had happened in the past so they could be friends again.

"Now, I believe that God has a plan for each and every one of us, and that He is truly the way, the truth, and the life," Dominic wrote.

To help you beat the emotional bullies that can push you to

do things you may regret, try using this simple step-by-step process the next time negative feelings hit you.

1. Mentally step into the space between your feelings and your response to them.

2. Take five deep in-and-out breaths to calm yourself while focusing on something that makes you feel peaceful and secure.

3. Think about the negative emotion and what triggered it. Separate how you felt about what happened from what really happened. Try looking at the situation from the viewpoint of the other person involved or from the perspective of an adult you respect and trust. What would an adult you look up to think about this situation? What would that person advise you to do?

4. Make sure you get a handle on where the negative emotion came from and why whatever happened triggered it. Did something in your past make the feeling more intense, or was the emotion based solely on this instance?

5. Create the most positive response you can make—one that will work out best for you over the long term.

6. Once you have the best possible response figured out, picture your negative emotions flowing out of you like heat or steam escaping your body and dissipating in the air.

7. Visualize yourself making a positive response and reaping the rewards.

8. Repeat this process every time you feel negative emotions come over you until it becomes your automatic response.

I've worked at this process myself, especially after I married Kanae and became a father. I want to be a good example to our son. I use my father and my uncle Batta as my guides when trying to figure out a better way to respond. They are very thoughtful men and good role models for me. I've been in business meetings with them where I've seen them control their responses in emotional situations. They always analyze things that affect their lives before acting on them.

> The negative things that happen to us don't have to rob us of our peace or our joy.

I want to be as mature as they are in that regard. Now that I have a family to look after, I feel more mature and I like that feeling. I have a better sense of who I am, the person I want to be, and what I want to do with my life. I am not so inclined to just get things off my chest or to vent—and that's good for everyone in my life.

More and more I realize that the negative things that happen to us don't have to rob us of our peace or our joy. You and I can make the decision to step into that place where we recognize our negative emotions, examine why we are feeling the way we feel, come up with positive responses, and then do our best to be our best.

I've matured a lot emotionally in the last few years. I feel like I'm more aware of the triggers and sources of my feelings, and hopefully, I'm more thoughtful in how I respond to them. I realize that while I can't control how I feel, I can control how I act.

Another key to living with emotional intelligence is never to suppress negative feelings so that over time they simmer until they explode. That's not healthy at all. You can manage your negative feelings in the moment, but sooner rather than later you need to address them and find a way to release the negative energy. I give it up to God. Instead of responding emotionally, you can ask Him to help you respond spiritually. Pray for those who have hurt you, knowing that God is just and that if you do your best, He will do the rest.

Nick's Notes for Chapter Seven

■ Emotions like fear and anger are natural feelings that you can't control, but you can control how you act on those emotions.

The space between feeling an emotion and responding to it is critical. In that space lies the secret to self-control and emotional intelligence—two gifts that can help you be more successful, confident, and happy.

Eight

Rise Above

Develop a spiritual
foundation to help
you be at peace
and stay strong.

As a child, I couldn't understand why God brought me into the world without arms and legs. I'd always been told God didn't make mistakes and He loved all of His children, but I couldn't reconcile that with my disabilities.

For years I prayed for arms and legs and, if not for them, at least something that would help me understand God's plan for me. I turned to the Bible for answers, and one day I found a passage, John 9:1–3, that truly changed my life.

It said Jesus came upon a man who'd been born blind. One of the disciples asked Jesus, "Who sinned, this man or his parents, that he was born blind?" That same question had been dogging me. Had my parents done something to make God angry? Was I born without limbs as their punishment? Or was I being punished for some reason?

When I read the next part of the passage, I got the chills. Actually, it floored me. It was as if I, too, had been blind but then made to see. It quotes Jesus answering the disciples' question about the blind man: "'Neither this man nor his parents sinned,' said Jesus, 'but this happened so that the work of God might be displayed in his life.'"

From that moment on, I believed that God had created me for a purpose. I didn't fully understand what that purpose might be, but I had faith that He planned one day either to give me a miracle or to somehow perform miracles through me.

Finding that passage on the blind man really changed my life by changing my attitude. So when I began having problems with bullies, I again looked to the Bible for answers. I found two particular passages that seemed to offer a couple of different responses to bullying.

There is the familiar story in which Jesus said we should turn the other cheek when confronted with evil people trying to hurt us. But then Jesus didn't exactly do that in John 18:19–23 when a guard slapped Him in the face in response to His defiance of the high priest.

After being slapped, Jesus responded with even more defiance: "If I said something wrong...testify as to what is wrong. But if I spoke the truth, why did you strike me?"

In this case, Jesus seemed to be more confrontational, asking the guard why he had struck Him. Jesus did not turn the other cheek, but He didn't strike back either. What I took away from this was that you could defend yourself against bullying without seeking "an eye for an eye."

I took this to heart a few years later when dealing with a school bully who was making my life miserable. I shared this story in my second book, *Unstoppable*. It wasn't easy telling the story in that book, which was the first time I shared it publicly.

I don't relish writing about it here either, but teens can relate to the anguish this bully Andrew caused me. This story is especially appropriate when discussing the role your faith can play in dealing with bullies and other challenges, which is another reason why I'm sharing it again.

In case you didn't read that earlier account, I'll give you a briefer version of it. But you should know that the thing Andrew kept saying to hurt me is a little graphic; so if you feel you might be offended, you can skip the next few paragraphs.

I know Andrew's bullying is not the worst form of bullying, because he never laid a hand on me. But at the time, I lived in constant dread of seeing him in the hallway—and I saw him at least once every day at school.

He was a year older than me, and it's entirely possible that he didn't think of himself as a bully. Often that's the case with certain bullies. They think they are being funny or just teasing, but those on the receiving end find their words hurtful, embarrassing, and intimidating.

Keep that in mind if you ever find yourself "just kidding" someone who is obviously not enjoying your humor. You might have unknowingly stepped into the bully role because you were insensitive or just unaware that what you were saying was hurtful to the other person. Everyone has sensitivities. You may think teasing a girl about her curly hair is funny, but maybe she finds it hurtful and mean. So if you tease people and they don't laugh or they look hurt, knock it off, please!

Andrew didn't stop. He was unrelenting. For about two weeks, every time he saw me at school, he would yell the same hurtful thing at me: "Nick has no d***!"

> If you tease people and they don't laugh or they look hurt, knock it off, please!

His taunt was very crude, meanspirited, and hurtful, even if it wasn't true. I knew it wasn't true, but of course no one else in school did. Wasn't it bad enough that I had no arms and no legs? Why did Andrew have to go around saying that?

It just seemed extremely cruel. It also irked me that other kids laughed when he said it. I had a pretty solid group of friends by that time. Most of the kids in the school knew me, and I got along with nearly everyone. Yet nobody stood up for me, and that seemed cruel too.

I would actually get sick to my stomach every morning just thinking about going to school and running into Andrew in the hallway. I tried to duck him, but our class schedules always seemed to put us on the same path at the same time.

Finally, I decided that I had to do something, because Andrew didn't appear capable of stopping on his own. He was like a parrot that had been taught only one sentence and just repeated it over and over. So one day, instead of trying to duck him in the hallway, I drove my wheelchair right at him.

Panic seemed to flash in his eyes for a second. Maybe he thought my chair was equipped with a missile launcher. That would have been sweet! (Not that I advocate violence in any form, of course.)

"Why do you do that?" I said to Andrew.

"Do what?" he replied.

"Why do you tease me and say that?" I asked.

"Does it offend you?"

"Yeah, it hurts me every time you say it."

"I didn't realize that, man. I was just kidding around. I'm sorry."

I studied his face for a couple of minutes to make sure he was being genuine. Honestly, I don't know what I would have done if he'd told me to get lost or taunted me again. But what I said next seemed to have a greater impact than anything else I could come up with.

"I forgive you," I said.

I don't think Andrew was expecting that. He bowed his

head a little. I'd like to think he felt shame or at least remorse for hurting me. Then he walked out of my life and never taunted me again.

If you've ever been bullied like that, you probably know how I felt. It was such a huge relief. I actually felt like I'd received a new set of lungs because it was so much easier to breathe. My stress level dropped dramatically. No more mornings of dread and fretting before school.

I thanked God for guiding me. I felt better about myself too. I was David. Andrew was Goliath. At least that's the way I'd felt in facing this nemesis. I hadn't exactly turned the other cheek. Instead, I'd looked into the bully's eyes, told him he was hurting me, and asked him to stop.

That approach worked for me on this occasion with this particular bully; I can't guarantee it will work for everyone in every situation. I'll offer some alternative methods for dealing with bullies in a later chapter. For now, my point is that you can rely on your faith for guidance and strength in dealing with the challenges in your life.

FAITH WORKS

I believe in the power of faith, and I encourage you to arm yourself with it. My campaign of faith against bullying takes me around the world. I often travel to countries where the governments or factions are hostile to Christians and the sharing of the gospel. Still, brave believers do as my grandparents did. They meet privately in Christian fellowship, reading God's Word together, knowing that they could face dreadful consequences if they openly displayed their love of God.

I am grateful that the authorities in these regions have shown me favor and allowed me to speak in their countries, sharing my message of hope and encouragement. As I travel to these places where many are hostile to Christians, I cling to the mandate from the apostle Paul in Ephesians 6 and "put on the whole armor of God" in order to protect myself from "the schemes of the devil."

> I believe in the power of faith, and I encourage you to arm yourself with it.

Paul said, "For we do not wrestle against flesh and blood, but against the rulers, against the authorities, against the cosmic powers over this present darkness, against the spiritual forces of evil in the heavenly places" (Ephesians 6:12).

Putting on the whole armor of God against these high-level bullies, I travel in safety. I wear the breastplate of righteousness, fasten the belt of truth around my waist, put on the helmet of salvation, and wield the sword of the Spirit.

I am grateful that God has opened unprecedented

opportunities for me to speak in places otherwise closed to Christian evangelism. I do my best to make the most of this access by encouraging all men, women, and children and radiating the love of Jesus. I show them that a man without limbs can live with joy through Jesus Christ.

It works for me, and it can work for you. I know because people tell me in person about the power of God in their lives, and every day we receive e-mails like this one from a young woman in Africa:

> After hearing about Nick and actually seeing him when he came to our church…I thought about all the excuses I had all my life. I was born with tiny slit eyes and due to that I was called names in school. I was insecure and not happy at all. I now live a very happy fulfilled life in Christ Jesus, with no excuses at all. I pray that Nick's message would reach out to the ends of the world to change the way we think and allow us to live fulfilled lives. I surrender to be used by God to spread His goodness all over to heal broken hearts and bring smiles to people's faces and hope in their hearts!

E-mails and letters like that help remind me that I have a purpose on this earth, just as you do. Many victims of bullying have written to me to say that their faith has helped them. I've heard from teens dealing with illnesses, disabilities, broken homes, addictions, and other problems. All have offered similar testimonies about the power of faith in their lives.

A sixteen-year-old from Scandinavia, who said he shares my Serbian heritage, wrote to tell me that praying had really helped him overcome depression and suicidal thoughts: "Whenever I have a hard time, I think...that God loves me and that He has a plan for me," he wrote. "My faith is much stronger now than it was before, thanks to you, and I'm also putting my faith into action now."

BULLIED BY EXPECTATIONS

As noted earlier in this chapter, some of the most extreme forms of bullying are cultural and even political in nature. As I've traveled around the world, particularly in Asia, I've met teens who've felt bullied by the expectations of others, including their parents and government leaders. I've been invited to speak to teens in these countries because the rate of depression and suicide is so high. I often encourage these teens to look to God for help in these situations, and many have written to tell me that their faith has saved them.

Camellia is one of them. She grew up in China, where a small portion of the population is Christian and there are few opportunities to learn about God. She didn't know any

Christians, but as a teen, she heard that the Bible was the number one best-selling book in the world, and that made her curious. What was it that made the Bible so popular?

She read the Bible and was inspired by the power of Jesus and His love for all people, but Camellia still couldn't find the faith to believe in God's existence. She spent her teen years doing what was expected of her—earning high marks in school. As she reached her late teens, though, she felt a void in her life. She felt she'd always lived according to the expectations of others, following their vision of what she should do without thinking about what she wanted.

Camellia's hard work had paid off and she was on course to achieve the successful life that her parents wanted for her, but she felt lost and depressed. Like so many young people, Camellia felt bullied by the expectations others had set for her. She wanted to choose her own path in life, and she wanted to further explore her questions about God's existence. It is no surprise then that Camellia felt lost.

"Why can't I find myself?" she recalled asking herself. "Why can't I find my direction? What do I really want to do? Do I spend all my lifetime, just [doing] what other people think [of as] successful?"

Camellia fell into a depression and contemplated suicide, she wrote, "because I could not find the reason I lived in this world."

Just as Camellia was slipping into despair, her university offered her the opportunity to study in New Zealand for a year.

"I decided to go without any hesitation because I knew this was the last chance I could seize to change my life in another way," she said in her e-mail to Life Without Limbs.

The Chinese government doesn't allow its citizens to use YouTube, but it is available in New Zealand, and Camellia discovered one of my videos while studying there. She said my testimony of faith touched her heart and inspired her to return to reading the Bible. She also attended a Harvest event conducted by my friend Greg Laurie in New Zealand, where she met many Christians and was impressed by them and their faith.

Camellia gave her life to God a short time later. She began attending a Baptist church and joined a Christian life group. She decided to stay in New Zealand where she has created an "unprecedented happy life."

"I just want to say without God I couldn't have such a happy life. I'm so glad God chose me to be His follower."

This young woman overcame many obstacles to take control of her life and pursue her dreams. She did this on a journey of faith. Now she is passing on that blessing by showing that path to others. Camellia is one of the many young people I've met who give me hope that this world will become a better, more loving, and more faith-filled place where bullying and oppression will no longer exist. I'm grateful that she has shared her story with us, and I hope it inspires you as much as she has inspired me.

Again, I encourage you to wield your faith to defend yourself against bullies and oppressors of every kind, at every level. Do as I've done in my travels and follow the advice of the apostle Paul to "put on the whole armor of God."

Nick's Notes for Chapter Eight

- Faith is a wonderful thing, but only if you use it. So if you believe in God, put your faith into action in your own life and in service to others.
- Faith is a powerful shield against bullies and other challenges, so always be aware that you can "put on the whole armor of God" by asking Him for strength and support.

Nine

Bully
for You!

Know that as bad as
being bullied can be,
you can walk away
wiser and stronger
from every challenge.

am about to throw something on the table that may sound crazy to you at first. Just humor ol' Nick for a few sentences and hopefully this idea will begin to make sense to you. If it doesn't, I'll buy you a new car.

Just kidding! How about a pony?

Seriously, here is the idea I'm asking you to consider: What if you could find ways to learn and grow from being bullied? What if you took a bully's hurtful actions and turned them into lessons learned so that you became stronger, wiser, and more confident?

Am I freaking you out? Do you have this strong desire to throw cold water on me to snap me out of it?

I am not suggesting that anyone should want to be bullied or that bullies are actually benevolent instead of malevolent. (I love that word; don't you? *Malevolent.* It just sounds so mean.)

My suggestion that you could possibly turn the tables and use a bully's negative energy to create something positive for yourself is actually based on my own experiences with bullies, scriptures from the Bible, words of wisdom from people I admire, a few recent psychological studies, and finally, true stories shared with me by teens around the world.

So before you throw this book against the wall and declare that Nicky V. has lost his marbles, let me present this evidence, okay?

Gain Through Pain

First, let's look at the bullying experiences of a natural-born bully magnet. I've had only one physical attack from a bully that I can recall, and that was way back in grade school. I've been taunted, teased, insulted, mocked, and made the butt of bully jokes so many times I can't count them.

Okay, so what resulted from all that cruel bullying?

I'm still here. Not only that, I have a wonderful life and a rewarding career, a beautiful and spiritual wife, an amazing son, and awesome family and friends. I can honestly say that being bullied in grade school and high school forced me to become more responsible for my own happiness, more self-confident, more outgoing, more faith filled, and more mature in dealing with people of all kinds.

Now it's also true that initially I didn't handle bullying very well. In fact, early in my grade school years I became quite despondent and even suicidal as you may recall. But over time and with the help of those who love me, including my family and my Lord and Savior Jesus, I learned to use bullying instead of allowing bullies to use me.

As much as I suffered mentally and emotionally from each of these bully encounters, I learned to walk away a little stronger each time. Sure, I was embarrassed and intimidated for a time, but no one goes through life without embarrassment or intimidation now and then. In each of these instances, I learned something about life, about other people, and about myself. And there is something very rewarding about growing from adversity, don't you think?

I'm sure there must be some people who get through their teen years without ever feeling insecure, embarrassed, isolated, awkward, or less than perfect, but I've never met such a person. Have you?

> Isn't there something pretty cool about getting back up after being knocked down?

And isn't there something pretty cool about getting back up after being knocked down, about achieving victory after failure, about learning from our mistakes, about having a weakness exposed and working to grow stronger?

Think about this: aren't many of the greatest heroes in books, movies, and songs people who have been knocked down by bullies or by difficult circumstances only to rise and emerge stronger?

In the grade school incident, I was provoked into a fight and I was very, very lucky that I wasn't hurt. In the case of the high school bully, I was again lucky that when I confronted Andrew, he backed down either in shock or because he really didn't understand how hurtful his words were. And in the most recent incident, the drunk at the hotel was just acting stupidly, not bent on causing me harm.

I am particularly vulnerable, and I know that I've been fortunate to escape physical injury. I hope you never have to deal with a bully who attacks you, but I encourage you to learn and grow from every challenge.

THE SCRIPTURE

Whether bullied by cruel teens or by life itself, we are all tested throughout our lives. You and I can choose to be defeated by our challenges, or we can rise above them and take the opportunity to grow stronger mentally, emotionally, physically, and spiritually.

Count it all joy, my brothers, when you meet trials of various kinds, for you know that the testing of your

faith produces steadfastness. And let steadfastness have
its full effect, that you may be perfect and complete,
lacking in nothing. (James 1:2–4)

This Bible verse from James always makes me think of my parents who had prepared themselves for the joy of the birth of their first son only to be confronted by the shock of learning that I had come into the world without arms or legs. They've often told me about that moment of realization at the hospital and the many fears and concerns that sent them into shock and grief instead of joy, but I never fully grasped how they must have felt until after the birth of my own son.

Can you imagine how happy I was to present them with my boy, Kiyoshi, and see the joy in their eyes? Since that moment, I've reflected, and I'm sure my parents have too, on the long road we've traveled together. My parents at first had little hope I would survive more than a few days after my birth, but when I proved to be a resilient little kiddiewink, they still had to grapple with the question of the life awaiting their limbless baby boy.

By the time I was out of the crib and quite literally bouncing off the walls like a human pinball, my mum and dad were praying for strength, wisdom, and courage. My mother was a nurse, but neither she nor my father could find any other parents who'd raised a child quite like me. They had to do it on a wing and a prayer.

Me too. Once I left the protective cocoon of family and went off to school, I encountered for the first time those feelings of being different, weird, rejected, and bullied. It hurt. Many nights I'd lie in bed praying that I'd wake up in the morning with arms and legs. I begged God for that.

I'm still waiting for my miracle. You may be waiting for yours too. You may be dealing with a bully or bullies who've made your life miserable. Or maybe something else has knocked you down, taken all the joy out of your life, and made you wonder whether you'll ever see better days.

As lonely as you may feel, you are not alone. Whether it's in our teens or as adults, circumstances and people beyond our control can whup on all of us. You feel like it will never end. You can't see a way out. But as long as you don't give in to your darkest feelings, there is always a way out.

> As lonely as you may feel,
> you are not alone.

There were many times when I felt so low as a teen that I wouldn't go to school because I didn't want to deal with the stares, the cruelties, the shunning, or the assumption that just because I looked different I was inferior, stupid, or not worthy.

Other times, I felt depressed and angry because I couldn't change the way I was, or blame anyone, for that matter. In many ways, I felt bullied by God. I didn't understand that if God loved me, why did He make me so different? Why did He not want me to run like other kids, to throw a ball, to ride a bike? Of all the kids at school, I was the weird one. I felt like a burden to my parents, my brother and sister, my teachers, and my classmates.

As you know, I had moments of despair and depression that drove me to attempt suicide at a very young age, but thankfully I did not go through with it.

I often struggled with self-doubt and fears. Bullies preyed on me at that age, and that didn't help. Still, as I worked through adolescent insecurities, I eventually realized that God wasn't bullying me. He had not made a mistake named Nick Vujicic. Instead, God had created someone whose "disabilities" were actually gifts in disguise—someone whose challenges would prove to be sources of strength. God does work in surprising ways. Scripture says He uses the foolish things of this world to confound the wise.

As strange as it may sound, my lack of limbs left me both disabled and enabled. Consider this: my lack of limbs forced me to go through trials and create a life that has now led me to you! I'm hoping you think that's a good thing. I certainly do.

The bullies in my life did not mean to make me stronger, but they did; and my hope is that your bullies will make you stronger too. God gave me a passion for sharing my story and

experiences. I believe it's because He wanted me to help you and others cope with whatever challenge you are dealing with. Let God turn your bullies into a blessing.

Romans 8:28 says, "And we know that in all things God works for the good of those who love him, who have been called according to his purpose." God does indeed have a purpose for us all. If God can use me, He can use you!

That verse speaks to my heart and gives me the faith to understand there is no such thing as good or bad luck. Even the bad things that happen in our lives can be for our good if we don't let them defeat us but instead turn them into opportunities to gain strength and grow.

I have complete peace knowing that God won't let anything happen to us unless He has a good purpose for it. I completely gave my life to Christ at the age of fifteen after reading John 9 in which Jesus explained that He had allowed a man to be born blind "so that the work of God might be displayed in his life."

At first, I thought that meant God would heal me so I could be a great testimony of His awesome power. Later on, I was given the wisdom to understand that if we pray for something, and if it's God's will, our miracle will happen in His time. If it's not God's will for it to happen, then we know that He has something better in store for us. I feel God uses us in ways that are unique to our stories and the challenges we have overcome. So for every bully, every hurt, and every challenge you've survived, your life grows richer and your spirit grows stronger!

Philippians 4:13 says, "I can do all things through Christ who strengthens me." God has a greater purpose for your life than anything you can imagine. Now, try to imagine, once again, that God can turn your bullying experiences into a gift with lifetime benefits.

Words of Wisdom

The belief that adversity can make us stronger has been around for a long time. Here are just a few of the quotations I've found from philosophers, leaders, heroes, and other wise women and men:

> You don't develop courage by being happy in your
> relationships every day. You develop it by surviving
> difficult times and challenging adversity. —Epicurus,
> a Greek philosopher who was born 341 years before
> Jesus Christ

> All the adversity I've had in my life, all my troubles and
> obstacles, have strengthened me.... You may not realize
> it when it happens, but a kick in the teeth may be the
> best thing in the world for you. —Walt Disney, who

went bankrupt and had his first cartoon character stolen from him before he went on to create Mickey Mouse, Disneyland, and Disney World

Comfort and prosperity have never enriched the world as much as adversity has. —The Reverend Billy Graham, one of my personal heroes and one of the greatest evangelists of all time

Where there is no struggle, there is no strength. —Oprah Winfrey, who was bullied and abused as a child before becoming a multimedia star and billionaire

Most of the verses written about praise in God's Word were voiced by people who were faced with crushing heartaches, injustice, treachery, slander, and scores of other difficult situations. —Joni Eareckson Tada, one of my mentors who became a global evangelist and best-selling author after being paralyzed as a teenager

When adversity strikes, that's when you have to be the most calm. Take a step back, stay strong, stay grounded, and press on. —LL Cool J, the rapper, actor, and entrepreneur who was bullied as a boy and later became a bully himself before turning his life around

I could give you many more of these testimonials about using your bullies and other challenges as motivation and inspiration to create a better life, but I think you get the point. If you still have some doubts, I have one more bit of evidence that says the bullies who want to make you their doormat can become your steppingstones instead.

THE SCIENTIFIC RESEARCH

It may seem obvious that those who bully us are our enemies, but research psychologists have come up with evidence that suggests they may also unwittingly serve as our friends over the long term. If that's too hard to swallow, maybe we'll just call them *frenemies*.

> Many people say that their bullies
> gave them motivation to work harder,
> be better, and prove their value.

One nonscientific observation that seems to make sense is that while most people experience bullying at some point in their lives, they manage to survive and move beyond it. In fact, many people say that their bullies gave them motivation to work harder, be better, and prove their value.

Maurissa Abecassis, a psychologist at a New Hampshire

college, told the *New York Times,* "Friendships provide a context in which children develop, but of course so do negative peer relations.... We should expect that both types of relationships, as different as they are, present opportunities for growth." As someone who was driven to consider suicide as a kid, I sure don't want to make it seem that we shouldn't take bullying seriously or that it is in any way acceptable or a good thing to have happen to you. But throughout this book, I've been telling you that what the bully does to you isn't nearly as important as how you choose, in the end, to respond to it. That's what this research says too.

A school bully who picks on a lot of kids may actually help them bond together in their mutual fear or dislike, which can enhance their self-esteem and self-confidence, according to another study. A series of experiments by psychologists at UCLA found that middle school girls who "reciprocated a fellow classmate's dislike" scored higher in social competence ratings than their peers who stayed neutral, according to "Can an Enemy Be a Child's Friend?" a *New York Times* report by Benedict Carey in May 2010. In simpler terms, the mean girls in your class can inspire you to make friends with their other victims and develop people skills in the process.

Another take on the potential benefits of being bullied as a teen is that it prepares you for dealing with meanspirited, deceptive, and dishonest people as an adult. These people do exist, and you have to learn to spot them quickly and avoid them, or at least keep your contact with them to a minimum.

I led a sheltered life while growing up in a Christian home. My instinct when dealing with people was always to give them the benefit of the doubt, which I still think is a healthy approach. As a teen, though, I often went too far in my trust of people. If people took advantage of me or deceived me or didn't do what they said they would do, I tended to think there had been a misunderstanding on my part or a mistake. Eventually, I came to realize these people were bullies of another sort. They abused me by preying on my trusting nature. Over time, I learned to pay attention to my gut feelings about people whose motives were suspect.

Many bullies pretend to be your friends either in person or on the Internet. They may act all nice and friendly to lure you in, but later they stab you in the back, try to turn other people against you, or suddenly shut you out after they are done using you. Psychologists say that teens who experience that kind of bullying often learn from it and become more alert and less likely to be victimized as adults, when the stakes can be much higher socially and financially.

Again, I don't think anyone believes bullying is a good thing, and if we could eradicate it from the planet, I'm sure the world would be a better place. My point in examining the opportunities to benefit from bullying is to help you learn and grow from what otherwise would be an entirely negative experience. Many teens have talked to me or written to me about doing just that.

USING BULLYING TO BETTER YOURSELF

Sixteen-year-old Peter wrote that he'd been bullied since the seventh grade by classmates who said bad things about him and made fun of him. It didn't help that he was so shy he was having trouble making friends with girls.

"I was always a smart kid and got first place in my class until ninth grade. And they also bullied me for being smart and for studying and having fun learning things and for knowing so much. I became so depressed that I thought that I should just sit alone at home and never go out."

Peter at first let the bullying drag him down. "I started to believe that I'm just not good enough, that I can't be the 'cool guy' that everybody wanted me to be, that others don't like me," he wrote. "And what does my life mean if others don't like me?"

Peter let these concerns embitter him initially. He took the "eye for an eye" approach and "started hating other people and thinking that I am always right and that they are bad and started ignoring them or wishing they had never been in my life."

That didn't work out for him, Peter said. "For the next two to three years I've had the same kind of lifestyle, closed, lonely, with nobody to talk with or share my story with. Sometimes I was so low in my life that I considered suicide."

I've read that many bullies were once victims of bullying themselves, and that was the case with Peter. He figured if he couldn't beat bullies, he'd join them. "I started doing all the things they do: teasing, bullying, not studying, bad behavior at school, swearing, disrespecting people," he wrote.

When I was bullied, I never dreamed that other people were dealing with similar problems. The same happened with Peter. He felt alone. He didn't think anyone else would understand his feelings. Then he met a girl who opened up to him about her own depression and isolation. Her trust made Peter feel trustworthy.

> **Many bullies were once victims of bullying themselves.**

They struck up a friendship. At first, Peter's insecurities got in the way, but this girl reached out to him and let him know she cared about him.

"That was when my journey of rebirth began," he wrote. "From then on I started realizing that if I was able to make that one girl smile with only a few words, then I could do anything in my life. So I began being me, and I started talking more and more to God and in a couple of months I realized that LOVE is the driving power of the world."

Peter recalled something that he'd heard me say in a video: "Never lose faith in God.... Just because you don't see God, it doesn't mean that He isn't there."

He wrote that his life has changed radically since he stopped trying to be like those who bullied him. Instead, he uses what he's learned from that negative experience to create a more positive life for himself.

"I am proud of who and what I am, what I accomplished and what good I did in this world. I am more open now. I am not as shy as I used to be. I can talk to anybody freely. I can understand, forgive and love any- and everybody," he wrote.

As he opened his heart to others, Peter found that they responded to him. Even those who had bullied him became his friends.

"People who have actually hated me at some point love me now because I have changed and I can love them as well.... And God has also gifted me with amazing friends who accept me how I am and just don't care about how I look or what I can and can't do," he wrote. "Now I know that I am beautiful, that I am special, that I have a purpose in this life and I will never give up."

Peter's first response to bullying was to buy into the negatives. He let bullying drag him down, and he even became a bully himself. That happens all too often. There is another choice, another path you can take, and thanks to the girl who befriended him, Peter found it.

He rejected the negative self-image that bullying had given him. He realized that he was a child of God and therefore was worthy of love. That seems like a simple thing, yet look at the results. He was no longer isolated. He found a girl who cared about him. The people who had bullied him became his friends. He wrote that some people even brought their own concerns to him for advice because he had grown so much in their eyes.

I believe the same can happen for you. Don't let a bully turn you into a victim. Instead, make the choice to turn a negative into a positive. Reject the bully and accept God's love. Use His strength to build a better life. Join Peter and me in saying, "I refuse to let a bully make my life worse. Instead, I will use this experience to make my life better than ever before!"

Nick's Notes for Chapter Nine

■ Believe it or not, there are ways to benefit from every negative experience, even bullying. So when dealing with a challenge, remind yourself to focus on what you can learn from it to make yourself stronger.

When dealing with a bully or other negative experience, keep in mind the words of James 1:2–4: "Count it all joy, my brothers, when you meet trials of various kinds, for you know that the testing of your faith produces steadfastness. And let steadfastness have its full effect, that you may be perfect and complete, lacking in nothing."

Ten

Create Your Bully Defense Strategy

Prepare yourself to successfully handle your bullies.

Three bullying experiences stand out as the worst in my life so far. The first was in grade school when a bully who wanted to beat me up pushed me into an epic playground battle. It ended when I surprised him—and myself—with a leaping headbutt that bloodied his nose and sent him fleeing from my life forever.

The second major bully encounter, which I mentioned earlier in this book, was in high school when an older classmate kept yelling the same crude thing at me every day in the hallway until I finally told him he was hurting me and asked him to stop.

The third was the most recent incident. My wife and I were staying at a nice hotel and enjoying the pool when a drunk walked by and made stupid and crass comments about my body. I just ignored him until he stumbled back into the hotel.

Each one of those incidents was hurtful. The first two stressed me out because the intimidation went on for what seemed like a long time. I still feel a little queasy when I recall how those first two bullies got inside my head. The third incident was over more quickly, but the fact that it happened in front of my new wife was embarrassing.

In looking back at each of those incidents, my response to bullying was different in each of them.

The first time, I allowed the bully to lure me into a fight.

The second time, I ignored the taunts for a while but finally confronted the bully verbally.

> My advice is to always avoid
> a fight if you can help it.

The third time, I just ignored the bully until he went away.

Honestly, I really didn't have a prepared strategy in any of those instances. I winged it, and fortunately it worked out. Each bullying situation we face is somewhat unique, and as I said earlier in this book, there is no single perfect way to deal one-on-one with bullies. My advice is to always avoid a fight if you can help it.

In my only fight with a bully, I escaped serious injury only out of dumb luck. I shudder to think what could have happened if he had been more violent or if he'd had a weapon. Even though we were very young, fights can escalate into deadly violence at any age. I know of several young people who have died in fights; some of them were killed by just one punch. So please do your best to stay out of fights with bullies.

If you have to protect yourself, there are ways to do that too. So far I've tried to give you a solid foundation for dealing mentally, emotionally, and spiritually with bullying. Now I want to get down to the nitty-gritty on what to do if you are confronted. There may come a time when you are face to face with a bully intent on causing you physical or emotional harm. So it's best to be prepared.

To protect yourself, I recommend creating a bully defense strategy that will help you remain calm and handle the situation as best as possible. Before we look at creating your personalized strategy for dealing with bullies, please review and read through the following Bully Defense System statement that reflects the material we've covered so far.

Bully Defense System

- Bullies can't hurt me or define me because I have defined myself. I know who I am and where I am going.
- I don't give anyone else the power to make me feel badly. I take responsibility for my own happiness.
- My values are unshakable. I have a plan for my life guided by them.

- My strength comes from within, and no bully can make me feel insecure.
- I know my family and friends will always stand up for me, just as I will for them.
- I am aware of my emotions, especially anger and fear, and I control my response to them so that I stay positive in my thoughts and actions.
- My spiritual life is strong and empowering. I know I was created for a purpose and I am loved unconditionally. Where I am weak, my Creator is strong.
- I find something positive to take away from every challenge, including being bullied.
- I reach out to help others at every opportunity, especially those who are being bullied in any way.

THE BASICS
OF A BULLY DEFENSE

You should feel confident, secure, strong, supported, and balanced as you read the Bully Defense System statement. When you truly believe it, you really are well equipped to deal with bullies. Now let's look at how you can respond to them as wisely and safely as possible.

How you respond to a confrontation with a bully depends on many factors, including your comfort levels with physical and verbal responses, whether you've had self-defense training, whether you or the bully have friends present, whether you can get help or reach safety quickly, and other variables.

For example, if a bully threatens to beat you up in an alley with no one else around, your response would need to be a lot different than if the threat came in a school hallway with teachers, administrators, and other potential allies nearby.

Still, there are a few basic rules that apply to any bullying confrontation, so let's look at them first. These are rules you can follow and steps you can take to prepare yourself if you think a confrontation is coming, so that you can act wisely and in a safe manner.

BULLY DEFENSE STRATEGIES

1. Assess the Situation

Before anything happens, consider whether the bully is a physical threat or just trying to scare or hurt you. It's best not to overreact, but it's better to overreact than to not be careful enough. If you know this bully is capable of causing you serious physical harm, you should talk to an adult, whether it's a parent, relative, teacher, coach, minister, or police officer. If you are certain that this bully just wants to embarrass you or harass you, it still would be a good idea to let an adult know you are having this problem, but you should also prepare yourself to stand tall and let the words bounce off you. Remember, you have a safety zone where you can go mentally and emotionally to be out of reach of hurtful words.

2. Call in Your Backup

If you think a bully plans to confront you at school, on the street, at a game or some other event, tell your parents and at least one other adult in a position to help you. You should also tell your friends. There is no glory in going it alone. If it is possible to always have at least one other person with you, try to do that. The people who care about you want to be there for you. Even if they can't be there when the bully confronts you, it is important to let them know that you feel threatened and to tell them who your bully is.

3. Stay Chill

Easier said than done, I know. If you think a confrontation is coming, read through your Bully Defense System statement a couple of times a day to build your confidence. Take some time to go through the scenarios of what might happen so you are mentally and emotionally prepared in the same way an athlete prepares for a game or match. Again, do your best to keep friends and supporters close.

If the bully confronts you, one of the best ways to stay calm is to control your breathing, taking longer breaths and slowly releasing them. If you've heard this bully's taunts before, try to take the sting out of them by picturing his words bouncing off you. They are only words after all. Sticks and stones, right? They only have the power to hurt if you allow that to happen. You have the power to just ignore them.

Your best first move might be to make no move at all. Ignore the bully's words. You should look at your antagonist, but don't get into a staring contest. Instead, acknowledge the bully and just keep walking. Most bullies thrive on getting a reaction that brings attention to them and feeds their egos. If you refuse to play that game, the bully might just decide you aren't worth picking on.

4. Tap into Your Faith and God's Strength

It's always good to have someone known as the almighty Lord watching your back. You are a child of God, and He will guide you through your battles. Draw upon His love.

> It's always good to have someone known as the almighty Lord watching your back.

5. Stand Tall

Bullies are less inclined to pick on someone who appears confident, so even if you don't feel that way inside, do your best to project that image on the outside without being cocky or aggressive. You can do this by looking at the bully, keeping your shoulders square and your chest back. When a bully taunts you, do not show emotion if you can help it. Many bullies will give up if they can't provoke a strong reaction to their nastiness.

6. Know Your Battleground

Train yourself to look around and assess the scene where a bully confronts you. Check to see whether the bully has friends nearby, whether there is anything you can use to defend yourself if you have no other choice. During your encounter with the bully, stay alert and be aware of changes in the bully's mood, tone of voice, and body language. If the bully grows more aggressive and moves toward you, be ready to walk or run away, call for help, or defend yourself.

Map out possible escape routes. Look around to see whether there is anyone nearby who might help you. Don't be afraid to ask strangers for help as a last resort. You can also just go stand by an adult to discourage the bully from attacking you. If you have a cell phone, make sure you program into it a quick-dial code for an emergency number for friends, family, or the authorities.

7. Respect the Bully

Sounds crazy, right? Some people become bullies to mask their insecurities and low self-esteem, so insulting them or putting them down may only turn a bad situation worse. As difficult as it may be, try to treat the bully with respect even if you aren't getting any in return. The bully's mood may be out of your control, but you don't want to add fuel to the flames.

8. Stay Out of Reach

The Bible offers some wise advice on bully avoidance in Proverbs 4:14–16, which says, "Do not enter the path of the wicked, and do not walk in the way of the evil. Avoid it; do not go on it; turn away from it and pass on. For they cannot sleep unless they have done wrong; they are robbed of sleep unless they have made someone stumble."

Hard to improve on that bit of ancient wisdom, right? It may seem obvious, but you should try not to go anyplace where your bully can confront you alone. If there is a playground or shopping mall or some other place your bully frequents, stay away. If your bully is confronting you at school or someplace else where you have to be, please try to keep as much distance between you and the bully as possible, especially if there is no one else around to help you.

Self-defense experts advise staying at least two or three steps out of reach. I advise you to stay two or three miles away if possible! You don't want to make it easy for the bully to grab you or to get in your face verbally. If the bully tries to close the distance, you have the options of retreating at a brisk walk—don't run if you can help it—or you can ask respectfully for the bully to stay back. If you walk or run away, make sure to keep checking to make sure the bully is not pursuing you.

9. Do Not Allow the Bully to Get You Alone or Take You Away from Others

If the bully attempts to push or drag you away from other people or into a vehicle, do your best to make as much noise as possible while resisting physically. Tell the bully to stop. If the bully doesn't listen, then yell "STOP!" as loudly as you can and try to get the attention of people around you.

It may be time to fight back if the bully continues to hold on to you. You might also fall down on the ground, grab a pole or a fence, and scream for help if you feel you're in danger of the bully dragging you off. Kicking, biting, scratching, and gouging are last-ditch self-defense moves if you feel you are under attack and in serious danger. If you have pepper spray, wasp spray, or a similar self-defense repellent and know how to use it, this would be the time.

YOUR PERSONAL STRATEGIES

I wish there was one perfect plan for dealing with all bullies. Maybe we'll have an antibully lightsaber one day. Until then, only you and your parents or trusted advisors can help you figure out what you are comfortable with and the best re-sponses for your particular situation. Some bullies are very aggressive and will escalate their attacks if you challenge them or try to reason with them. Others may back down, leave you alone, or sneak up on you at another time. You have to read them carefully, and then there is the fact that some are just unpredictable.

All you can really do is try to plan for each possible scenario so that you are prepared for whatever comes. I know I've said this before—probably several times—but please make sure you let an adult you trust know that there is a bully on your tail. Tell the adult who the bully is, the nature of the bullying, and where it occurs. If something happens, you want to have some-one who can help your family find you. Again, hope for the best, but prepare for the worst.

> Identify at least five adults who could help you deal with your bully problem.

To help you figure out how to best respond to your bully, I've prepared some questions that you can think about and an-swer in a journal or on separate sheets of paper. By thinking through your responses now, you will be calmer and more con-fident if a confrontation occurs. And even better, you'll have a plan to hightail it out of there.

Here are some things to consider for your beat-the-bully strategy:

- Are you more confident simply ignoring a bully's taunts, or do you want to stand up to the bully and respond?
- Do you think you can convince your bully to leave you alone through persuasion or humor?
- Is your bully likely to become violent?
- Is your bully more inclined to come at you alone or with a group of friends?
- Do you know of anyone, adult or teen, who could persuade your bully to leave you alone?
- What about having your parents, a teacher, or a mutual acquaintance contact your bully's parents and ask for help? Is that an option?
- Identify at least five adults who could help you deal with your bully problem. Set up times to speak with each of them, ask for their advice, and listen to their suggestions.

Your Response Options

Another important thing to think about before your nemesis comes stalking you is what you should and shouldn't say in response to cruel taunts or comments. Again, this is very much a matter of personal preference based on your comfort level. If you are quick witted and a fast sprinter, you may be comfortable making wisecracks and jokes or even slamming the bully with your own teasing and taunts.

If that's the tactic you want to use, I hope you can run like the wind, or at least faster than the bully. (I have a fast wheelchair; you can borrow it if you'd like. No wheelies though!)

It might be helpful for you to identify just what type of bully you are dealing with before planning your response. Here are some options for specific types of bullies.

THE UNINTENTIONAL OR NONHOSTILE BULLY

One of the weird things that comes with the Nick Vujicic No Arms, No Legs Appearance Package is that certain people will say hurtful things to me because they don't know how else to respond to me. They don't mean to be hurtful; they just say the first thing that pops into their heads, make a dumb joke, or say something that they think is only gentle teasing but is really more hurtful than that.

Remember when you were little and you "liked" someone in your class so you pinched that person or threw a ball at them or knocked them down on the playground? Well, that's sort of what happens to me *all* the time. When I was younger, it really knotted my knickers sometimes that people could be so insensitive, but as I've grown older, I've come to understand that some people are just awkward or lack basic social skills when it comes to relating to someone with a disability. It's also true that I often tell jokes about being "armless but not harmless" and make other wisecracks at my own expense, so people sometimes try to come up with their own versions. They don't mean to be mean, but it comes across that way.

The same can be true of certain bullies. Some are not malicious people bent on ruining your life—even though that's what they seem to be doing. In some cases, classmates or acquaintances may think they are being funny or "just teasing" you, but it's more hurtful than they realize.

Even stranger, sometimes a person who wants to get to know you better will tease you or make rude comments just to get your attention. If you think that could be what's going on with your bully, then try to show the person that your feelings are being hurt. Asking the bully to stop making rude comments worked for me once or twice, but be aware that bullies with a heart or a conscience are fairly rare. If your bully is truly mean as a snake, the response you get may be, "You think I *care* that I hurt your feelings, *you fool*!"

Hopefully your bully isn't a sociopath. Here are a few suggested phrases that might hit home if your antagonistic bully has any heart at all:

- "I don't think you realize how much your

comments hurt me. I'd appreciate it if you'd stop picking on me."

- "You know, I've heard you're really not a bad person and neither am I. Could we try to get along? I am not enjoying this."

- "You may think you are just teasing me, but I'm feeling bullied by you, so could you ease up on me? I'm having a rough time with this stuff."

- "If I did something to offend you or hurt you, could we talk about it? I really don't want there to be any bad feelings between us."

- "I was talking to some friends about the way you are treating me and they can't understand why you have singled me out. Can we talk about this and find a way to move past it?"

- "I know you think what you are saying is funny, and I get it, but I'm sort of sensitive about that particular thing, so I'm asking you to please stop saying it to me."

THE HOSTILE BULLY

If your bully's role model is the serial killer on television's *Dexter* or the murderous dude from all of those *Halloween* movies, you probably won't have much luck appealing to the person's conscience. In fact, you'll want to say something that will allow you to get away as fast as you can. If the seriously hostile bully comes after you, here are some basic nonconfrontational, passive phrases to use as you make a hasty retreat:

- "Okay, I understand. I have to go meet with my teacher now. See you later."
- "My father is waiting for me, so I have to go. Catch you later."
- "Sorry you feel that way. I wish you didn't. Now I have to go meet the assistant principal. Bye."
- "You seem upset and I'm not helping, so I'll just go meet my friends down the street and maybe we can talk later."

It can be helpful to let the bully think friends are waiting for you and they would come looking for you if the bully caused problems, so mentioning something along those lines is recommended if you are dealing with a serious threat.

THE SOCIAL BULLY

If your bully is one of those mean girl or mean guy bullies whose preferred form of torture is trying to exclude you or to convince others to shun you by spreading rumors or lies about you, there is probably less risk of the bully turning violent. But you can probably expect your bully to resist if you attempt to join the bully's social circle. The social bully may have convinced others to shun you too. It's sad, but the pack mentality can be tough to overcome.

My suggestion is not to beat your head against that wall. Instead, I'd recommend that you try getting to know the members of this crowd individually and win their acceptance one by one—or maybe just look somewhere else for friends. The "in crowd" or the "popular kids" may not be all that nice when you get to know them. You might discover that they really aren't much fun to be around as individuals or collectively.

I made the mistake of trying to fit in with a crowd when I was a teen. Even when they sort of accepted me, there was still something awkward about it. Okay, that something was me! I was awkward because I was not acting like myself. Don't make that mistake. Don't give up who you are just to fit in. Instead, find friends who accept the real you.

> It's a lot more fun to hang out
> with people who accept you.

The best bet is usually to find your own friends naturally, by being yourself and letting people discover the wonder of you. Look for those who share your interests and have compatible personalities. It's a lot more fun to hang out with people who accept you rather than always trying to fit in with people who are constantly judging you.

I'll never forget the teenage girl who stood up during one of my first speeches and asked if she could come hug me. Then as she gave me a hug, she whispered in my ear, "Thank you. No one has ever told me that I am beautiful before." Oh man, I nearly lost it! So sad!

We all have insecurities. We all want to be accepted. If you've been struggling, just know that it will get better. The teen years are the toughest. I promise. You will find a much more welcoming world out there than the one you may have known in high school. In fact, over the years you may even discover that the social cliques from high school break up and you become better friends with your former classmates as adults.

The reason so many people struggle with loneliness and feel that they don't fit in during the teen years is—this may sound a little strange—because so many people are struggling and feeling like they don't fit in during their teen years.

Insecurity runs rampant for teens. When all the people around you are trying to figure out who they are and struggling for acceptance, it creates this crazy environment where nearly everyone is fighting for social survival. As a result, there are very few people with the confidence just to say, "I love everybody and everybody can love me. And if you don't love me, well, that's your loss!"

Don't you wish you could feel that way? Well, you can! And you might be amazed at what happens when you accept yourself and let others discover just how wonderful you are. One of my friends has a teenage daughter named Jeannie who had a very difficult time after moving to a new town and a new school. She'd grown up in a smaller town where she'd had many friends. She didn't know anyone in the new and much bigger high school.

Her father told me it broke his heart when Jeannie came home from her first day at the new school and said she'd eaten lunch all by herself and cried because she felt so alone. There was a group of girls who seemed to be a lot of fun, but whenever one of them wanted to invite Jeannie to a birthday party or a dance, a girl named Laurie said she didn't like Jeannie. Laurie was a bully. She was a pretty girl, but she saw Jeannie as competition because the boys were beginning to notice her. She also didn't like the fact that Jeannie was a really good singer and the choir director had praised her instead of Laurie.

Jeannie was hurt at first. She cried a lot about being shunned by Laurie and her crowd. But then she did something very brave. She decided that her parents were right when they said she should just let other kids figure out how cool and fun she really was. So Jeannie stopped trying to fit in with Laurie's crowd. Instead, she was just her usual friendly, fun self. She relaxed.

"Let people come to you," her mother said.

That is what Jeannie did, and it worked. Soon, she had her own big circle of friends, both boys and girls. And do you know what happened? Jeannie and Laurie ended up going to the same college. They even joined the same sorority, where Jeannie became a leader. One day, Laurie told her that she hoped they could be friends and maybe even roommates when they graduated.

Jeannie could have turned into a bully herself at that moment. Instead, she told her former bully, "That would be great!" And she meant it. Jeannie won! She did it by trusting in herself, sticking to her values, and just focusing on being a nice person. Her self-confidence and natural charm worked their magic and drew people to her. She even won over Laurie, who eventually realized that she'd been wrong to exclude Jeannie from her social circle.

THE CYBERBULLY

One of the saddest and sickest stories I've heard in a long time is the news report of a girl in Washington, DC, who committed suicide because she'd been bullied online. The worst part was that even on the day of her funeral there were cruel comments made about her on Facebook. How heartless can a bully be?

The really tragic thing is that there are so many similar stories like this. If you don't believe me, try Googling teen suicides caused by online bullying. It is very scary to see what pops up, and it should be a warning to everyone that cyberbullying is as bad or worse than other forms of harassment.

Cyberbullies send threatening e-mails, texts, and tweets. They also post their taunts online and spread rumors about people on social networking sites. Some even post unflattering pictures of their targets or pretend to be someone else online so they can manipulate their victims, blackmail them, or set them up to be embarrassed.

Many cyberbullies do their dirty work anonymously. If you feel threatened and fear that someone is stalking you online or somehow trying to hurt you emotionally or physically by posting in social media, texting, or tweeting, the first thing you should do is save all the e-mails or website posts made by your online bully. That is your proof that someone is harassing you.

Show all the materials to your parents and any other adult you can trust so they can help you decide what to do about the person. The one good aspect is that cyberbullies leave tracks that can be preserved and presented to authorities so the bullies can be traced and, very often, prosecuted or at least shut down.

Online bullies have many methods, and their tactics and tools are constantly evolving with new technologies, social media, and websites. Cyberbullies may set up websites, chat rooms, message boards, blogs, or social media pages to impersonate you, spread rumors about you, blackmail you, or harass you. They may put embarrassing photos or videos of you on the Internet or even create them to subject you to ridicule.

One way to make yourself a big target of cyberbullying is to get caught up in sexting, which is a bad idea in so many ways. Sexting involves sending sexually explicit text messages or photos to another person. Why people do this is beyond me. It is a recipe for disaster, and it dishonors the body God gave you. In 1 Corinthians 6:19–20, we're told that our bodies are temples "of the Holy Spirit, who is in you, whom you have received from God," and we are told also to "honor God with your body."

I've been informed that in many cases girls who feel pressured to have sex with boyfriends will sext them instead, hoping that will be enough. My response to that is to ask why you would want to be with someone who cares only about your physical appearance or having sex with you. You should be secure enough to find someone who loves you for what is in your heart, not simply for how you look or for just sexual pleasure. There is so much more to a relationship, which is why I favor abstinence until you are married to someone whom you truly love and trust.

Please think about the long-term consequences of your actions before you sext. I've heard about teens who've sexted images of their bodies, thinking they were just sending the photos or messages to a boyfriend or girlfriend only to have bullies or enemies get hold of their sexts and send them out all over Facebook, MySpace, and other social media.

There is no Undo button for this. Once an image goes out on the Internet, it is there forever—for anyone to see. If you are ever tempted to engage in sexting, think about whether you want your parents, grandparents, siblings, ministers, or teachers—or someday your children and grandchildren—to see those photos or messages! What would you tell your own kids if they knew you'd sexted as a teenager? How embarrassing would that be?

> Once an image goes out on the
> Internet, it is there forever—
> for anyone to see.

The consequences of sexting can be long lasting and serious. Teens have lost their jobs as well as their positions in organizations and honor societies. They've also hurt their chances for getting accepted to colleges. Some have seriously damaged their reputations because of sexting.

There's also the fact that in many areas law enforcement officials consider sexting a form of child pornography, so that anyone who sends it or receives it could possibly be charged with engaging in that unlawful practice.

Protect Yourself on the Internet

If you have the slightest feeling that someone is trying to hurt you or your reputation in any way on the Internet and through social media, preserve the evidence if you can, and then break the connection immediately. By that, I mean do not respond to the person's e-mails, texts, tweets, blogs, chats, Facebook posts, or any other form of communication. But, again, try to save them if possible.

This is a very serious issue around the world. Every week I hear stories of young people committing suicide or turning to drugs and alcohol because of cyberbullying. There are several websites manned by volunteers that will help you track and stop an online bully. One of the oldest is www.wiredsafety.org. They offer information on how to find out the identities of anonymous cyberbullies so that you can give their names to your parents, school officials, or police.

Do not give out any personal information or engage with the online bully in any way. Most of all, *never* agree to meet in person—especially alone—with someone you've met online. At the first hint that someone is cyberbullying, cyberstalking, or trying to intimidate, harass, or get information from you online, save their e-mails, texts, and tweets as evidence, and then please alert your parents, guardians, teachers, or law enforcement.

Many states now have antibullying laws, and some are aimed specifically at online or electronic bullying. You can block cyberbullies' texts and e-mails and keep them from posting to your Facebook page. You may have to create new accounts under a different name to prevent further attempts. Don't let online bullies or any bullies take away your peace of mind and self-esteem. Be strong! If you find yourself obsessing over things being said or sent to you online, talk to your parents, friends, or trusted teachers, counselors, or church leaders.

Many online bullies don't realize that cyberbullying is against the law, so if you feel harassed or threatened, you or your parents can go to the police and report it. The Cyberbullying Research Center is a great resource for dealing with this type of bully. It is run by a couple of college professors who are experts on this topic: Dr. Sameer Hinduja of Florida Atlantic University and Dr. Justin Patchin of the University of Wisconsin-Eau Claire. They have a very helpful website at cyberbullying.us, which offers the following guidelines.

Preventing Cyberbulling: Top Ten Tips for Teens

1. Educate Yourself
To prevent cyberbullying from occurring you must understand exactly what it is. Research what constitutes cyberbullying, as

well as how and where it is most likely to occur. Talk to your friends about what they are seeing and experiencing.

2. Protect Your Password

Safeguard your password and other private information from prying eyes. Never leave passwords or other identifying information where others can see it. Also, never give out this information to anyone, even your best friend. If others know it, take the time to change it now!

3. Keep Photos "PG"

Before posting or sending that sexy image of yourself, consider if it's something you would want your parents, grandparents, and the rest of the world to see. Bullies can use this picture as ammunition to make life miserable for you.

4. Never Open Unidentified or Unsolicited Messages

Never open messages (e-mails, text messages, Facebook messages, etc.) from people you don't know or from known bullies. Delete them without reading. They could contain viruses that automatically infect your device if opened. Also never click on links to pages that are sent from someone you don't know. These too could contain a virus designed to collect your personal or private information.

5. Log Out of Online Accounts

Don't save passwords in form fields within websites or your web browser for convenience, and don't stay logged in when you walk away from the computer or cell phone. Don't give anyone even the slightest chance to pose as you online through your device. If you forget to log out of Facebook when using the computer at the library, the next person who uses that computer could get into your account and cause significant problems for you.

6. Pause Before You Post

Do not post anything that may compromise your reputation. People will judge you based on how you appear to them online. They will also give or deny you opportunities (jobs, scholarships, internships) based on this.

7. Raise Awareness

Start a movement, create a club, build a campaign, or host an event to bring awareness to cyberbullying. While you may understand what it is, it's not until others are aware of it too that we can truly prevent it from occurring.

8. Set Up Privacy Controls

Restrict access of your online profile to trusted friends only. Most social networking sites like Facebook and Google+ offer you the ability to share certain information with friends only, but these settings must be configured in order to ensure maximum protection.

9. Google Yourself

Regularly search your name in every major search engine (e.g., Google, Bing, Yahoo). If any personal information or photo comes up that may be used by cyberbullies to target you, take action to have it removed before it becomes a problem.

10. Don't Be a Cyberbully Yourself

Treat others how you would want to be treated. By being a jerk to others online, you are reinforcing the idea that the behavior is acceptable.

Your best defense against bullies of all types is knowing and believing that you are God's creation. You have value and you are loved. No bully can take those things away from you. God created you for a purpose, and He has a plan for you. A bully will try to bring you down and make you feel bad about yourself, but you can make the choice to reject anything the bully says or does. Instead, look to those who love you and to your Creator for strength and inspiration.

And don't forget me! I'm always here for you too!

Nick's Notes for Chapter Ten

- Every coach has a game plan. Every general has a battle plan. Everyone who is bullied should have a plan too.

- Taking the time to prepare for your bully and the situation you are dealing with can make a huge difference. If you prepare yourself ahead of time by planning your responses and your escape methods, as well as lining up backup, you will have a lot more confidence and less fear when your bully shows up.

- You should always tell at least one adult you trust if you feel threatened, trapped, manipulated, or isolated by a bully. You don't have to handle it on your own; in fact, you should ask for help as soon as you feel threatened or stressed. Even if the adult can't do anything about it, you should have someone who knows there is a problem in case anything happens to you.

Eleven

Stand Up to Stop Bullying

Be a good Samaritan and help eradicate the bullying epidemic.

When someone asked Jesus, "Who is my neighbor?" He told a story about a Jewish man traveling from Jerusalem to Jericho who was robbed, beaten, and left for dead on the road. Two people, a priest and a Levite, passed by without offering any help, but a third man, who was from Samaria, went to his aid despite the fact that Samaritans and Jews were enemies in those times.

The Samaritan treated the Jewish man's wounds and took him to a hotel where he cared for him. Before leaving, the Samaritan gave the innkeeper money and promised to return to check on him.

After telling the story, Jesus asked His listeners to identify the true neighbor among the three who came upon the beaten man. When someone responded that it was the Samaritan because he alone had mercy on the victim, Jesus said, "Go and do likewise."

In this book, I've provided you with a bully defense system

because I love you and I want to do everything I can to protect you from emotional and physical harm. Now, in this final chapter, I want to encourage you to "go and do likewise."

I encourage you to develop empathy for others, like the good Samaritan showed. Please do everything you can to protect others from emotional and physical harm caused by bullies.

I am hereby deputizing you as a modern-day good Samaritan. Your mission is to do everything within your power to stamp out bullying anywhere and everywhere. I know you are just one person. I'm just one person too, and I'm one person who is short four limbs! Yet I've traveled the world encouraging and convincing teenagers to make it uncool to be a bully. You can do likewise in your own school, family, neighborhood, community, state, and country.

Stand together so no one will stand alone!

Bullies try to isolate and prey on people; so if we stand together against bullying, that can never happen. Stand together so no one will stand alone! Wouldn't that be wonderful?

Bullying is a global issue, and it has a negative impact on the quality of our lives. Bullies rob young people of their joy. They terrorize them and turn schools and playgrounds into places darkened by fear and dread. I nearly took my life because of bullying. I know others who did take their lives and still others who turned to drugs, alcohol, and injuring themselves to alleviate the pain.

Experts on bullying say it also creates a vicious cycle of violence. Many of those who've been bullied in the past become bullies themselves. The violent people who conducted several of the most infamous mass shootings in schools and other places were reportedly once bullied. We can stop this cycle by working to identify bullies in our midst and doing whatever it takes to change their behavior and help them find a new path.

For a time as a teenager, I hated my life because of bullies at school. I can understand the rage inside those bullied people who become bullies themselves. But I also understand there is a way to disarm that rage and to find a much better way to live, one that is illuminated by God's love.

You see, I discovered that while you can hurt and be hurt with words, you also can heal and save with words. The Bible says we are "fearfully and wonderfully made." Armed with that truth, we can fight bullying by assuring each and every person we meet that we are all children of God, loved by Him and deserving of His best.

So now that you are equipped with your bully defense system, how do you join our global campaign against bullying? Here are a few suggestions, and feel free to add your own:

- Make it your mission to be on the alert for bullying in any form and to do whatever you can safely do to stop it.
- If there is not an antibullying program at your school, go online and find out how to start one—there are scores of websites, including the US government's www.stopbullying.gov, which is devoted to the topic. Then meet with your school administrators and student representatives to put one in place. Most antibullying websites give instructions for starting petitions and fund-raising drives to create antibullying programs.
- Suggest that your school, church, service group, club, or community sponsor a showing of the very well made and moving documentary *Bully* (2011) during October as part of National Bullying Prevention Month. The film captures fully the pain of those who are bullied, but it also is inspirational because it offers ways we can all take a stand to stop bullying.
- Start an online bullying report program so that people who witness or experience bullying in any form can report it anonymously and get the help they need to stop it.
- Talk to your friends and classmates about bullying

and its impact on you as well as the toll it has taken on others around the world. Then ask them to join you in stamping out bullying and being a good Samaritan at every opportunity.

- Use your Facebook page, Twitter account, and any other social networking connections to spread the word that bullying is not cool and that anyone who is being bullied or witnesses bullying should report it and follow up to make sure it is stopped.

I promise that you won't be alone in your efforts to stop bullying. Thousands of people around the world have committed to end this epidemic, and I know for a fact that God is already at work. Each week, there are more and more antibullying campaigns around the world. I applaud local, state, and national governments that have enacted legislation against bullying. But we can't rely just on elected officials and government agencies. This should be a cause embraced by everyone, because bullying impacts us all.

People of faith in particular need to step up and become the advocates—the modern-day good Samaritans—for victims. Jesus was the supreme role model for standing up to bullies and in teaching us how to respond to bullies. Christ was reviled by bullies who had it out for Him. And yet He never lashed out. He never stooped to their level. With compassion, Jesus dealt with bullies from a platform of love and redemption.

Jesus said, "You are the light of the world. A city on a hill cannot be hidden.... Let your light shine before men, that they may see your good deeds and praise your Father in heaven." Please join me in this never-ending effort to stand up and stop bullying in every form it takes and wherever it may occur in the world. Reach out to victims and potential victims, and help them develop their own bully defense systems.

As a father, I will serve as the champion defender for my son. I do not want him to be the target of a bully's reckless comments, but I cannot isolate him in a protective bubble. He will one day feel the sting of someone's deliberate arrows of cruelty. And to prepare him, I will spend plenty of time coaching my son on how to neutralize the comments from an angry peer.

Our antibullying campaigns can begin within our own families as we protect those we love, but if we are to be true good Samaritans, our loving protection should extend to everyone faced with bullying.

Together let's embrace, support, and protect those targeted by bullies. Help them build their own bully defense systems. Together let's wipe away the tears of those who privately struggle. Together let's rise up to protect the wounded hearts of boys, girls, men, and women around the world, the very same people for whom Christ gave His life. And finally, let's work together to make this a safer, more peaceful, kinder, and more loving world for the next generations of teens—our children and their children too!

Okay, it's time to go out and conquer bullying. To help you do that, I'm posting your Bully Defense System statement again on the next page, at the end of this book, so you can easily find it. I hope you will read it and use it as often as you feel it will help you. I love you!

Nick's Notes for Chapter Eleven

- Be a good Samaritan and reach out to anyone who is being bullied.
- Stand up against bullying in your neighborhood, your school, and your community so that no one stands alone in dealing with a bully.
- Break the cycle of bullying. If you have been a victim, don't turn around and bully someone else.
- Even if you haven't received the miracle you seek, be a miracle for someone else!

Bully Defense System

- Bullies can't hurt me or define me because I have defined myself. I know who I am and where I am going.

- I don't give anyone else the power to make me feel badly. I take responsibility for my own happiness.

- My values are unshakable. I have a plan for my life guided by them.

- My strength comes from within, and no bully can make me feel insecure.

- I know my family and friends will always stand up for me, just as I will for them.

- I am aware of my emotions, especially anger and fear, and I control my response to them so that I stay positive in my thoughts and actions.

- My spiritual life is strong and empowering. I know I was created for a purpose and I am loved unconditionally. Where I am weak, my Creator is strong.

- I find something positive to take away from every challenge, including being bullied.

- I reach out to help others at every opportunity, especially those who are being bullied in any way.

Resources

Nick Vujicic
Life Without Limbs, www.lifewithoutlimbs.org
Attitude Is Altitude, www.attitudeisaltitude.com
Nick's Facebook page, www.facebook.com/nickvujicic

The US Government's Antibullying Website
www.stopbullying.gov

The Antibullying Website for PACER (Parent Advocacy Coalition for Educational Rights)
www.pacerteensagainstbullying.org

The Cyberbullying Research Center
cyberbullying.us

For Tracking Cyberbullies
www.wiredsafety.org
www.cyberangels.org

Acknowledgments

Once again, I thank God: the Father, Son, and Holy Spirit.

My wife, Kanae, is my greatest blessing, my comforter, and my shield against all of life's challenges. Thank you for loving me, spending your life with me, and blessing us with our son. My wife is a gift that I was prepared to receive only because my mum and my dad guided me so thoughtfully through my childhood and into adulthood. They helped me become a man of God worthy of such a woman, and they gave me a foundation of strength to be the husband and father my family deserves.

My writing collaborator and dear friend, Wes Smith, again helped me convey my message of hope to the world in this book, as he has done in all of them, for which I am very grateful. The other key members of my publishing team are Jan Miller and Nena Madonia of Dupree Miller & Associates literary agency, who also have become great friends and supporters. Also my deepest thanks to my publisher, WaterBrook Multnomah, a division of Random House, and its professional team, including Gary Jansen, Steve Cobb, and Bruce Nygren.

Finally, thanks to our staff, board, and team at Life Without Limbs and Attitude Is Altitude, and especially to you, my readers and to all of those who have written to me to share their stories of inspiration, hope, and faith—particularly those whose stories we've used in this book. We love receiving your posts, letters, and e-mails. Your feedback inspires me, and your stories sustain me. I love you all. God bless you.

About the Author

NICK VUJICIC is an evangelist, a motivational speaker, and the director of Life Without Limbs, an organization for the physically disabled. Born with severe physical disability (he has no arms or legs), Nick has nonetheless become a great inspiration to people around the world, regularly speaking to large crowds on overcoming obstacles and achieving your dreams. A frequent subject of media coverage, Nick has been interviewed by ABC TV's *20/20,* the *Los Angeles Times,* TBN, *The 700 Club, Life Today, Joni and Friends,* Janet Parshall, Joel Osteen, *Family Talk,* and many others. A longtime resident of Australia, he now lives in Southern California with his wife, Kanae, and son, Kiyoshi.

What would your life be like if *anything* were possible?

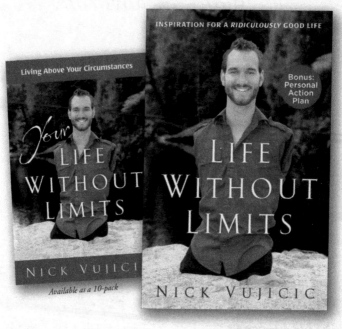

Nick tells the story of his physical disabilities and the emotional battle he endured while learning to deal with them as a child, teen, and young adult. Nick shares how his faith in God has been his major source of strength, and he explains that once he found a sense of purpose—inspiring others to better their lives and the world around them—he found the confidence to build a rewarding and productive life without limits. Let Nick inspire you to start living your own life without limits.

Read an excerpt from this book and more at
www.WaterBrookMultnomah.com!

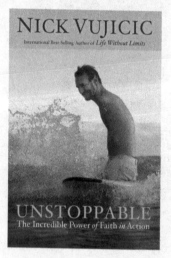